SLAVERY AND THE CHURCH.

BY

WILLIAM HOSMER.

"IT IS A DEBT WE OWE TO THE PURITY OF OUR RELIGION, TO SHOW THAT IT IS AT VARI-
ANCE WITH THAT LAW WHICH WARRANTS SLAVERY."—*Patrick Henry.*

NEGRO UNIVERSITIES PRESS
NEW YORK

Originally published in 1853
by William J. Moses, Auburn, N.Y.

Reprinted 1969 by
Negro Universities Press
A DIVISION OF GREENWOOD PUBLISHING CORP.
NEW YORK

SBN 8371-1646-5

PREFACE.

HAVING been engaged, for several months past, in a newspaper controversy on the subject of slavery, and having a desire to prolong, as well as to deepen, the impression of truth, the author has deemed it incumbent upon him to present his views to the public in a more systematic and permanent form. He flatters himself that his sentiments, when understood, will be found to have no other ultraism than that of truth, and no other tendency than that of righteousness.

It is made our duty to "weep with those that weep," and to "remember them that are in bonds, as bound with them." The example of the Samaritan, who relieved the man that fell among thieves, is commended to our notice by the injunction, "Go and do thou likewise." It would doubtless be easier for the present, to pass by on the other side, like the Levite, and leave the forlorn and wretched uncared for; but in that event, what becomes of Christian principle? and what of fraternal feeling?

That a large number of the inhabitants of this Republic — more than one-eighth of our entire population — have been robbed of every personal, social, civil, political and religious right,

and are at this moment exposed to sale in the market, like cattle — is no secret.   But when this outrage is charged upon its
perpetrators as a crime, the public are informed that no wrong
has been done — that Christianity sanctions the act.   Believing
that this allegation is wholly unfounded, and that Christianity
no more sanctions slavery than it does other high crimes, the
writer has endeavored to express his dissent plainly, but can-
didly, and with such argumentative force as patient thought and
thorough conviction have enabled him to command.

CONTENTS.

———•———

PART I.

THE MORAL CHARACTER OF SLAVERY.

CHAPTER VII.

CHAPTER VIII.

PART II.

THE RELATION OF SLAVERY TO THE CHURCH.

CHAPTER I.

CHAPTER II.

CHAPTER III.

PART III.

DUTY OF THE CHURCH IN RELATION TO SLAVERY.

CHAPTER I.

CHAPTER II.

CHAPTER III.

CHAPTER IV.

CHAPTER V.

CHAPTER VI.

CHAPTER VII.

CHAPTER VIII.

CHAPTER IX.

SLAVERY AND THE CHURCH.

PART I.

THE MORAL CHARACTER OF SLAVERY.

CHAPTER I.

SLAVERY DEFINED.

IT is important, in the outset of this discussion, to ascertain the exact meaning of the term Slavery. Many have appeared as the defenders of slavery, who never would have done so, had they admitted the full import of the word. They have narrowed down the meaning of the term until — in their own imagination — it was reduced to a defensible point, and then, with great industry, endeavored to construct arguments for its support. All this labor might have been saved, and the cause of truth not a little advanced, if they had adhered to the established use of words.

A slave, in the proper sense of the word, is one whose personal, political, civil, and religious rights have been swept away — one who may be bought and

sold, like any other property, and who is obliged to
obey the commands of a master, whether those commands are right or wrong.   Dr. Webster defines the
word slave as follows: 1. "A person who is wholly
subject to the will of another; one who has no freedom of action, but whose person and services are
wholly under the control of another.   The slaves of
modern times are generally purchased like horses and
oxen.   2. One who has lost the power of resistance;
or, one who surrenders himself to any power whatever, as a *slave* to passion, to lust, to ambition."   This is,
perhaps, the highest literary authority on the subject,
and it is in entire accordance with the slave laws,
both of our own and other countries, whether relating
to the present age, or to any former period.   A few
citations from slave laws, which are always the same
in substance, will settle this question :

"A slave is one who is IN THE POWER of the master to whom
he belongs.   The master may sell him, dispose of his person,
his industry, and his labor; he can do nothing, possess nothing,
nor acquire anything but what must belong to his master."
(*Laws of Louisiana, Civil Code, Art.* 35.)

"The slave is ENTIRELY subject to the will of his master."
(*Id., Civil Code, Art.* 273.)

"Slaves shall be deemed, held, taken, reputed, and adjudged
in law, to be CHATTELS PERSONAL, in the hands of their owners and possessors, and their executors, administrators, and assigns, to all intents, constructions, and purposes whatsoever."
(*Laws of South Carolina, Brev. Dig.,* 229.)

"In case the personal property of a ward shall consist of specific articles, such as slaves, working beasts, animals of any kind, stock, furniture, plate, books, and so forth, the court, if it shall deem it advantageous to the ward, may, at any time, pass an order for the sale thereof." (*Laws of Maryland, Act of* 1798, *Chap.* 61.)

The above quotations are a sample of the slave laws of every State and every nation. In some instances there may be more rigor, in others less, but slavery never exists in the absence of the above principles.

It is of slavery that we write — not of its abuses. To treat of the abuses of slavery, would be as absurd as to treat of the abuses of any other high crime. Hence, our reference to the slave code is sparing, and embraces only a few of its most approved and unquestioned principles. What possible enormities are, or have been, engrafted upon these principles, is comparatively unimportant, since the system, under any conceivable administration, would be utterly intolerable. It is not for us to talk of incidental and contingent horrors attendant upon guilt — it does not become a grave, ethical discussion to take advantage of such things. If slavery, in its most common and blameless character, is not wholly vile and altogether beyond endurance — if it be not one of the highest crimes ever committed by man — then we yield the ground at once. We have no wish to take advantage of any accidental evils connected with slavery. A good system might be abused, but the abuses would not prove the system bad. In discussing the moral character of an act, we only wish to know what the

act is in its most simple form. Were we discussing
the moral character of murder, we should not wish to
encumber the subject with any special cruelties which
might have taken place at some particular time; we
should only want to know what murder is in its nature — in its most common and least exaggerated
character. We have to do with the substance of slavery, and not with its incidents.

There are three elements of the slave system wholly
inseparable from it — three characteristics of the slave,
which distinguish his condition from that of all other
persons :

1. The slave is under the entire control of his master.

2. The slave is property — a chattel, real or personal.

3. The slave is a perpetual, unconditional, hereditary servant.

Of these in order.

Absolute Subjection.

The entire supremacy of the master is absolutely essential to slavery. The system could not exist
if this main pillar were removed. Masters claim,
and the law gives them, entire control. Slaves must
do what they are bidden, be it right or wrong, or
suffer any punishment their owners see proper to
inflict. The law recognizes no right in the slave to
resist the master in anything — no, not even in de-
fending his own life or virtue. It is true, the slave
laws of this country do not directly authorize the
master to take the life of the slave at pleasure ; and

in this respect they are perhaps better than the slave laws of ancient Greece and Rome ; but all slave owners indirectly have this authority. They may command the slave to do what they please, and kill him if he disobeys — that is, whip him to death for stubbornness, or shoot him for alleged resistance. As no slave is allowed to be a witness in any case against his master, or any other white person, it is impossible to bring the offender to justice, unless he has had the indiscretion to commit the offence before a white person. The slave has not one religious or civil privilege guaranteed to him. In respect to everything of this kind, he stands before the law, not as a human being, but as a brute, to be disposed of according to the will of the owner. Blackstone truly calls this power "absolute and unlimited," and considers it essential to the idea of slavery :

" Pure and proper slavery does not, nay, cannot, subsist in England : such, I mean, whereby an absolute and unlimited power is given to the master over the life and fortune of the slave. (*Comm., Book* i, *Ch.* 14.)

It would be well if the law went no farther, but it even lays the master under disabilities : he may not emancipate the slave, nor pay him wages, nor elevate him by education ; that is, the law will not permit either of these things without embarrassment, and some of them it wholly prohibits. Thus, while the master has all authority for evil towards his slave, his authority for good is seriously abridged. It follows, therefore, that slavery is not only an absolute personal despotism on the part of the master, but a malignant despotism — it may never relax into justice or generosity. The law may, or may not authorize special barbarity; but it never gives to the master less than entire and undisputed authority over the slave. Hence, where such control is wanting, we cannot denominate the condition slavery — it is not slavery, whatever else it may be.

Slaves are Property.

The slave is unquestionably property, and nothing but property — a chattel — so claimed by all slaveholders, and so designated by all slave laws. By this one provision he is stricken from the human, and classed with the brute. He ceases to be a man, and takes rank with cattle. He is mere property — a thing to be bought, and sold, and possessed, as freely and truly as a horse or an ox, or any inanimate chattel, as, for instance, a watch or a wagon. It is not merely the slave's services that are owned, or bought, or sold in this manner; no — it is himself — his body and soul, with all their powers and capabilities. It is the man converted into a *thing*, that constitutes the article of traffic. To man, as man, belong certain inalienable rights; but to man, as a slave, belongs nothing. His flesh, and bones, and spirit, and life, are the property of another. He is a chattel personal, and liable to all the chances of property, like any other chattel. He has not even the right to life. His master may be forbidden to kill him, but the slave has no right to remonstrate against

being killed. This feature of slavery is considered by
Mr. Barnes as the chief characteristic of the institution. It is, however, but one of the characteristics
of slavery; there are other things equally fundamental, although such ownership as the master has in
the slave is wholly unknown to any other relation in
life. The husband possesses his wife, but she is not a
chattel; parents possess children, but they are not
chattels; masters have servants, but servants are not
chattels: in none of these relations is there anything
analogous to this feature of slavery. It is slavery,
and slavery only, that strips a man of humanity so
completely as to make him take rank with articles of
merchandise.

Slaves are Servants.

Some have endeavored to show that slavery consists in mere servitude.

"I define slavery," says Dr. Paley, "to be an obligation to
labor for the benefit of the master, without the contract or consent of the servant." (*Mor. and Pol. Phil., Book* iii, *Ch.* 3.)

This is only a description of involuntary servitude,
and includes but a part of what is necessary to constitute slavery. Dr. Fuller, who tries to defend
slavery on the basis of this definition, is, therefore,
wholly at fault. Blackstone expressly affirms that
servitude may be perpetual, where slavery is not possible :

"A slave or a negro, the moment he lands in England, falls
under the protection of the law, and so far becomes a free-

man; though the master's right to his services may possibly continue." (*Comm.*, *Book* i, *Ch.* 1.)

Again: "It is now laid down that a slave, or negro, the instant he lands in England, becomes a freeman; that is, the law will protect him in the enjoyment of his person and his property; yet with regard to any right which the master may have lawfully acquired to the perpetual service of John or Thomas, this will remain exactly the same." (*Id.*, *Book* i, *Ch.* 14.)

It will not do, therefore, to make the idea of servitude alone, the representative of slavery, inasmuch as it comprehends only one element of slavery. By way of illustration, we may take the crime of murder, and define it thus — " killing a human being ;" or even thus, " willfully killing a human being." But would either of these definitions be correct? Not at all. And yet it is true, beyond all doubt, that killing a human being is essential to the crime of murder, as cognizable by our laws. The fact is, the above definitions include only a part of what is comprehended in the crime specified, and for this reason cannot be admitted as correct. The same is true of Dr. Paley's definition of slavery. He has defined what may be a crime, but not what constitutes the crime in question. The difference is this: all slaves are servants, but all servants are not slaves. Nor does the qualification — " without the contract or consent of the servant "— by any means embrace all the essential features of the slave system. A servant, though his servitude be perpetual, may be no chattel; his remaining personal rights may be secured by law as effectually as those of any other man, and his children may be free in all respects. But the servitude of the slave is perpetual, unconditional, and hereditary—it applies to him and all his descendants for all time, without any qualifications whatever.

Either the above is a just exposition of slavery, or we have no word in our language expressive of the condition of the unemancipated colored man in the Southern States. A servant he is, and that, too, under the most abject circumstances, but he is far more than a servant: he is a thing—a chattel personal, and the service which he performs is done, not with his own hands, for he has no hands with which to labor—his limbs belong to his master. He is more than a servant chattel—he is a subject of the most absolute despotism. The master's will is the slave's only law. He may heed no other command, whether emanating from God or man. It appears, therefore, that slavery is a term used to signify a complication of wrongs. It denotes one who is stripped of all but life, and whose life is held by a very uncertain tenure — the will of his master.

This is slavery as it exists among us, and as it has existed in all ages of the world. It is not an exaggerated picture, drawn for effect, but an exact and careful delineation of the system, as it stands recorded upon the statute books of slave-holding States. Nor are these laws in any respect a dead letter. They are everywhere enforced to the full extent, or at least as much so as any human laws. We never hear of the slave's becoming free through the inoperative char-

acter of the laws. His personal treatment may be
better or worse, but he is still a thing, and not a
man. His good treatment gains no legal immunities
for him, or his wife, or his children. Chattels they
are, and chattels they must forever remain, while under the slave law.

Our estimate of the system must be formed on the
basis of its entire character, and not on any of its
particular features. The parts separately may be
more tolerable than when combined. We shall, therefore, speak of slavery, not as it has been defined by
its apologists, but as it is — not as an ideality which
never had an existence, except in the mind of its in-
ventor, but as an actual institution, known and read
of all men. We readily admit, that the continued
introduction of what does not belong to the definition,
would vitiate it, just as certainly as do the omissions
which we have noticed in the definition of murder.
If we should define murder to be "killing a man
with malice aforethought, by burning him over a
slow fire," the definition would be faulty through
excess — it includes more than is necessary, and more
than commonly attaches to the crime of murder.
Just so with slavery : if we define it to be "an obligation to labor for the benefit of the master, without the contract or consent of the servant, and also to
be a chattel personal in the hands of the master, sub-
mitting, in all things to his sovereign, unlimited control, and receiving forty lashes a day" — the definition
will at once be pronounced incorrect, because the
forty lashes per day are not essential to the condition

of the slave, nor are they commonly inflicted. They may be inflicted if the master pleases, and so may the murderer burn his victim over a slow fire, or cut him into inch pieces. The definition we have given is based on the laws of the slave States, and on the entire history of slavery, as it now prevails, and has prevailed in all ages of the world. It is important to distinguish between slavery and serfdom, or ville-nage, or servitude. The latter have some of the ele-ments of slavery — just as excusable homicide has some of the elements of willful murder — but, as we never confound the different kinds of killing, so neither should we the different kinds of servitude. Let slavery stand upon its own merits, as defined by law, and by the common language of men, especially where its ethical character is under consideration. We have no right to pervert the meaning of the term, and then pronounce it either good or bad, according to our definition.

CHAPTER II.

SLAVERY A SIN.

As we have defined slavery, its moral obliquity ad-mits of no dispute, except among that class who be-lieve the slave was made to be a slave, and that he has no capacities or rights beyond what are provided

for in that abject condition.   But even those who base
their argument on the assumed inferiority of the slave,
must yield the point, or push their conclusions much
farther than they have yet done.   The humanity of
the slave must be denied, or the sinfulness of slavery
is evident.   Short of this extreme, the advocates of
slavery cannot stop; because the rights of man belong to man under every exigency of life ; they are
inherent in his nature, and cannot be separated there-
from by the arbitrary institutions of society.   Human
laws do not reach the endowments which we receive
from nature.   Manhood is prior to law, and therefore
always paramount when the claims of law and humanity come into conflict.

The sinfulness of Slavery is established by arguments drawn from the following sources:

1. The constitution of man.
2. The civil law.
3. The moral sense of mankind.
4. The Scriptures.

1. *The Constitution of Man.*

" Sin is the transgression of the law."   It is the transgression of any right law, whether divine or human.
The law of God is embodied in the constitution of his
creatures no less plainly than in the ten commandments
that were written upon tables of stone.   The nature and
faculties of man declare for what he was made, and
proclaim slavery a violence and an indignity offered to
the Creator's work.   The slave is a man, and hence,
justly entitled to be treated as a man.   He is a man,

and is obligated to perform the duties of a man. But slavery will admit of neither; it takes away all his rights as a member of the human family, and all his obligations as a creature of God. The following observations of Dr. Whewell bear upon both of these points with much force:

" As far as the limits of humanity extend, there are mutual ties of duty which bind together all men, and as the basis of all others, a duty of mutual kindness; which, as we see, is acknowledged by the jurists as well as the moralists of Rome, in spite of the originally narrow basis of their jurisprudence. The progress of the conception of *humanity*, as a universal bond which knits together the whole human race, and makes kindness to every member of it a duty, was immeasurably promoted by the teaching and influence of Christianity. In the course of time, domestic slavery was abolished; and marriage received the sanction of the church, and was alike honorable in all. The antipathies of nations, the jealousies of classes, the selfishness, fierceness and coldness of men's hearts, the narrowness and dimness of their understandings, have prevented their receiving cordially and fully the comprehensive precepts of benevolence which Christianity delivers; but, as these obstacles have been more and more overcome, the doctrine has been more and more assented to, and felt to be true, by all persons of moral culture; that there is a duty of universal benevolence which we are to bear to men *as men;* and which we are to fulfill by dealing with them as men — as beings having the like affections and reason, rights and claims which we ourselves have.

" This conception of humanity as a principle within us, requiring us to recognize in others the same rights which we claim for ourselves, may be further illustrated. Such a principle of humanity, requiring us to recognize men as men, requires us more especially to recognize them as such in their capacity of moral agents. They have not only like desires and affections with ourselves, but also like faculties of reason and self-guidance, by which they discern the difference of right and wrong, and feel the duty of doing the right and abstaining from the wrong. This view of their condition as moral agents, is that by which we must entirely sympathize with them; as it is the view of our own condition in which we are fully conscious of ourselves. Humanity requires that we should feel satisfaction in the desires and means of enjoyment of our fellow men; but humanity requires, still more clearly, that we should feel a satisfaction in their having the desires and the means of doing their duty. Now, the fundamental rights of which we have so often spoken, the rights of the person, of property, and the like, are means and necessary conditions of duty. It is necessary to moral action, that the agent should be free, not liable to unlimited and unregulated constraint and violence; that is, that he should have the rights of the person. It is necessary to moral action, that the agent should have some command over external things; for this is implied in action; that is, it is necessary that he should have the rights of property. And, in like manner, in order that any class of persons may exist permanently in a community, as moral agents, it is requisite that they should possess the right of marriage; for without that right, some of the strongest of man's desires cannot be under moral control; nor can the sentiment of rights be transmitted from one generation to another. The right of contract is a necessary accompaniment of the right of property; for, if the person can possess, he may buy and sell. And thus these rights are necessary conditions of men's being moral agents; and the humanity which makes us desire that all men should be able to regulate themselves by a love of duty, requires that all should be invested with these rights." (*Elem. Mor.*, *Book* iii, *Chap.* 23.)

The slave, being human, must be permitted to exercise the functions of humanity, or the end for which he was created is contravened. If he is to be degraded from manhood to a level with the brutes, his human endowments are superfluous, and ought to have been withheld. If his powers of thought are not to be exercised, if his sense of obligation is to be contracted to the single point of obedience to his master, and if he may neither possess anything, nor acquire anything, why were the faculties, the capacity for doing these things, conferred upon him? Was it intended that these powers should remain latent? or were they as evidently designed to be cultivated in the slave as in other men? The slave is a man, and has the right to be a man. This is the order of God with reference to him, and as plainly expressed as if it had been the subject of a special revelation from Heaven. Do we need a revelation to inform us what our hands and feet, our eyes and ears, were made for? Could a supernatural communication of that kind render their use any more apparent? Not in the least. Finding, then, man endowed as he is, the use of those endowments can no longer be questioned. If the eye was made to see with in one case, it was made to see with in all cases; that is, it was made to be used, and used according to its original design. To make a man throw aside his humanity and become a chattel, to blot him out from civil society, and remove from him every right which is peculiar to man — to do all this, is as clearly sinful as it would be to cut off the hands or the feet without cause, and even more so, because the intellectual, social and moral powers which slavery blights, are of greater consequence than the members of the body. In short, under the slave system, man cannot be man ; and this blight upon his powers, this necessity of sinking below the nature that God has given, is manifestly a perversion of that nature, and a sin against the primal law of his being.

2. *The Civil Law.*

Slavery is a perversion of nature, and can only exist by positive statute. This is admitted by slave-holders themselves. No man is born a slave, except as the civil law under which he is born declares him to be such. It is not remarkable, therefore, that all law is naturally against the institution. Slave legislation is special ; it is a departure from all the ordinary principles of law-making. The citation of authorities here can scarcely be necessary, since it is known to all that the sole design of law is to promote the welfare of men. Its objects are rights and wrongs — the enforcement of the former and the prohibition of the latter. Blackstone says the civil law is properly defined to be,

" A rule of civil conduct, prescribed by the supreme power in the State, commanding what is right and prohibiting what is wrong." (*Comm., Int., Section* 2.)

He further adds :

" Justinian has reduced the whole doctrine of law to these three general precepts: 1. That we should live honestly ; 2. Should hurt nobody ; 3. And should render to every one his due." (*Ibid.*)

Burke says, " law is beneficence acting by rule;" and

with this agree all writers on law. The civil law is, therefore, clearly on the side of the slave. If the institution of law bears upon him at all, it is bound by its very nature to do him good. The law should know him only for his benefit. And yet, strange to say, law is made the instrument of the complete and total subversion of all his rights. By law, he is driven from among men, and made to take rank with brutes. Thus an institution which professedly aims at the happiness of every man, becomes the direct occasion of immeasurable injustice. Slavery is the greatest possible outrage upon law; it destroys every thing that law was intended to preserve. I shall not here attempt to show the causes of this anomaly, but simply mark its atrocity. That people who cherish civil law, and who thereby profess to be aiming at protection and justice for all, should so far pervert law as to render it destructive of all protection and justice, is truly astonishing. The slave is a man, and claims, as rightfully as any other man, every advantage that can flow from the civil law. How men can sustain such law, and yet deny the colored man all participation in its benefits, is a mystery not easily solved. It is violating all the principles of law. If the negro is a man, he is entitled to protection, and to withhold it from him is an arbitrary and wicked departure from the avowed purposes of government. We see not how slavery can be regarded otherwise than sin, if the maxims of law are right, for it pours contempt upon them all. Instead of guarding, it robs; instead of sustaining rights, it tramples them in the dust.

3. *The Moral Sense of Mankind.*

Slavery is repugnant to the moral feelings. Law may be perverted till it sanctions the greatest crimes, but the moral sense of man must always condemn it. The slave is, or is not, a man; if the former, he has the same rights as other men; if the latter, his rights are only those of brute nature. Whatever the law may ordain in the case, conscience is inflexible. We must either cease to make moral distinctions — must abandon all ideas of right and wrong, as applicable to men, or else allow that the slave has the same rights as ourselves. There is no rule in ethics by which we can distinguish the rights of the white man from the rights of the colored man. Justice is the same to both; protection, liberty, happiness, and all other blessings are the same to man, whatever may be the color of his skin. If the law gives all power to one complexion and denies all to the other, then the law is palpably subversive of right — it is wanting in that attribute of rectitude which is essential to law.

Slavery cannot be made to agree with moral principle, except upon the gratuitous assumption that the slave is not human. In order to fasten chains upon the unoffending negro, we have to sever him from the brotherhood of man. This the moral sense will not admit, and hence slavery is of necessity branded as a crime.

4. *The Scriptures.*

It has been assumed by the supporters of slavery, that the institution is sanctioned by the Scriptures.

Indeed, they have claimed for it almost every kind of support, but we shall show now, and more fully hereafter, that slavery is not only not countenanced by the Bible, but absolutely prohibited. The question is not, whether some particular features of slavery ever had an existence under the sanction of Scripture, but whether or not the system of slavery, as it exists in this country and has existed in every country, and in every age, is so sanctioned. Servitude was allowed, but we have shown that servitude alone is not slavery. The purchase of a servant was allowed, but did not reduce the servant to a chattel. Beyond this, no one will presume to allege Scripture authority for the complicated abominations implied in the term slavery. On the other hand, the Scriptures pointedly assert the manhood of man, declaring that God "hath made of one blood all nations of men," and that "he is no respecter of persons." These declarations overthrow the only foundation on which slavery rests. As we have said, it is not possible in physiology, or law, or morals, to find a reason for enslaving a man; he must be presumed to be an inferior nature, before so great a calamity can he inflicted upon him. But Christianity sternly repels all ideas of inferiority as attaching to any particular race or class of mankind. Again, the Scriptures may not prohibit slavery in form, but they do so in *fact*, by enjoining holiness upon all men, and forbidding in detail the several sins which, in their aggregate, constitute the crime of slavery. Injustice is prohibited, and this prohibition strikes at the robbery practiced by the slave-holder, in denying the slave the rights which belong to him as a member of the human family. In like manner, unkindness, cruelty, neglect, and oppression are forbidden towards all men, and, consequently, towards the slave. But slavery could not exist, apart from these wrongs; it is made up of them, and falls to the ground when they cease. The Scriptures enjoin all kindness towards our fellow men, but slavery is opposed to kindness — it is ever studious of all unkindness to its victims. Once more, the Scriptures command us to love our neighbor as ourselves, but this cannot be done by him who denies his brother personal freedom and the rights of manhood.

But more than all, the obligations which the Bible lays upon every man, render slavery an utter impossibility. God claims supreme authority over every man, and has made it the duty of every man to obey him in all things. This limits the despotism of slavery. It also prevents the traffic in men. They cannot be chattels, and still be Christians. They have the duties of husband and wife, parents and children, to perform, and these duties, every one of them, are in open and eternal conflict with slavery. We therefore conclude that the Bible ignores the relation of master and slave, whatever it may teach respecting master and servant.

CHAPTER III.

SLAVERY A GREAT SIN.

THE conclusion that slavery is a sin — however clearly sustained — does by no means cover the whole ground. It is a sin, beyond doubt, but there are many who esteem it only a venial sin — such an one as is greatly palliated by the circumstances, having little or nothing of the enormity which attaches to crime. But all such notions are most unfounded. Slavery is not only a sin, but a sin of the greatest atrocity. It is an enormity in the moral world. It breaks every law of God, and every law of man — except the slave law. Not, indeed, if slavery is only servitude — not if we exclude despotism and chattelship. Were there nothing more than simple service required of the slave, and had he secured to him the rights of a man in all other respects, his condition might be tolerable, or, if not tolerable, yet much less intolerable than now, and, therefore, less guilty. Such mitigation is unknown — where slavery is, there man always is, and always must be, a chattel, " entirely subject to the control of his master." The degradation is total, and the sin proportionate.

The extreme criminality of slavery as compared with other infractions of law, lies in its cutting off the possibilities of happiness. It takes not singly — it invades not by degrees, but sweeps everything at once and forever. Other crimes usually assault us in detail, and rob or injure by piece-meal, taking here and there a little, clandestinely or otherwise, but leaving on the whole far more than they take. The most rapacious robber, if he spares life, leaves character and liberty, wife and children, health and hope. But the slave-holder takes all — person and property, wife and children, together with all their capacities and powers, for all time to come. Nothing is left to the slave, unless it be animal life, and that is his — or rather in his possession, for his master's use — only on the most precarious terms. Common robbery is undoubtedly a great crime, yet, contrasted with slavery, it sinks into utter insignificance; it is a fault so venial that it scarcely deserves censure. Theft is a crime, but what other thief ever stole as the slave-holder steals? He takes the man and all his present and future acquisitions. Oppression is a sin, yet no mere political tyrant ever crushed humanity in so grievous a manner as the slave-holder. The worst of rulers never claimed to sell his subjects as he would cattle — never made them articles of merchandise, and trafficked in them without restraint — never forbid their marriage, or owning property, or becoming citizens. But slave-holders do this, and do it according to law. Our laws declare the foreign slave trade to be piracy, and punish it with death, but the domestic slave trade, which is every way as bad, they uphold with all the strength of the government.

Thus it is clear that slavery is equivalent to a combination of all the worst acts known to the penal code of civilized nations, if we except the single crime of murder. And even this exception can hardly be made, because the slave's life has no adequate legal protection. Hence it is no exaggeration to pronounce the system the "sum of all villainies." It amounts to this by the most sober calculation. All rights that the law could or should have protected are destroyed, by putting the individual beyond the pale of society. All that civil law would have made his, is thus taken from him and given to his master.

But this grand act of spoliation only reaches to the temporal relations of the slave. As if to enhance the wrong to the uttermost, the tie which binds man to his Maker is severed as far as it can be by human authority, and the master takes the place of God. No slave has a right to perform any act of worship without the consent of his owner. He may not keep the Sabbath, nor hear the gospel preached, nor pray, nor confess Christ. For him, there are no means of grace but such as his master may choose. If the master chooses none, the slave must submit or suffer any punishment his owner sees proper to inflict. The rights of conscience are unknown to slavery. The slave is supposed to have no conscience ; his whole duty being to obey in all things, his owner or any one whom his owner may appoint. Here, then, is a human being divested of all right to obey his Creator in the performance of those high duties which are enjoined equally upon every man. It is not a simple curtailment of religious liberty, but — if the master so orders — a total abnegation of the right of worship. The law has provided not the smallest

fraction of relief for the slave's conscience, however
sorely oppressed. What is such a system but pre-
meditated spiritual murder? It is the complete
abandonment of the soul as well as the body to the
unrestrained authority of any person whom the slave
is obliged to call master. Now, if the slightest interference with our obligations to God is a sin, what
shall we say of a system that cuts off all obligation
forever? If to coerce the conscience even in a few
particulars, is an offence too great to be tolerated,
how enormous must be the crime of trampling the
moral faculties in the dust, as though they formed no
part of our nature? To style such a system wicked,
conveys no adequate impression of its monstrous
character. Wicked it is, but more so, infinitely, than
any ordinary form of vice. It is a transcending, all-
pervading usurpation; it leaves not a vestige of spiritual or temporal power to those on whom God has
laid all the duties of humanity. It assumes the responsibility of blotting out not single rights, but all
rights of every kind, leaving the whole man as much
a blank as he would have been, had the creating hand
denied him every human endowment.

It is tame to call such a frightful outrage, wrong.
There wants a name in language sufficiently strong
to characterize an evil of this kind. We are not ac-
customed to view man apart from law, and the crimes
which he commits and the injuries he suffers are mostly
violations of some single law; but in the case of the
slave we have no such rule; he is in a state of legal desolation. · No man can commit a crime against him, nor

can he commit a crime against any man. If he is killed, it is not murder. If he kills, it is not murder. He
is not indictable for any offence. The law knows him
not, except as the property of his master; stripped of
all protection, save as property is protected, he stands
an outcast from the human family. What additional
wrong has society to inflict? All that law could
have made his, is taken from him by putting him
beyond the operation of law — the law, in fact, is
not only broken at a single point, as in ordinary crime,
but broken at all points, and removed out of the way,
that it may never more oppose a barrier to the master's rapacity. If even a single violation of a righteous law is wicked, what must be the enormous wickedness of a system that is not contented with solitary
infractions, but destroys the very existence of law?

These considerations place the system in the list of
highest crimes. There is no law but the slave law
that it does not break — none that it does not utterly
destroy. It is a pure, unmixed sin, scorning isola-
tion or selection, and like the Angel of Death, carrying indiscriminate destruction wherever it goes.

CHAPTER IV.

SLAVERY A SIN UNDER ALL CIRCUMSTANCES.

THE advocates of slavery have strangely asserted
that the guilt or innocence of slave-holding depends

upon circumstances. This is to place slavery where it does not belong, among things pure in themselves, and vicious only by abuse. Dr. Fuller thus states the case :

" The enormities often resulting from slavery, and which excite our abhorrence, are not inseparable from it — they are not elements in the system, but abuses of it. What is slavery? ' I define slavery,' says Paley, ' to be an obligation to labor for the benefit of the master, without the contract or consent of the slave.' This is all that enters into the definition of slavery, and now what ingredient here is sinful? Suppose a master to render unto his servant the things that are just and equal; suppose the servant well clothed and religiously instructed, and to receive a fair reward for labor in modes of compensation best suited to his condition; might not the Bible permit the relation to continue, and might it not be best for the slave himself? Recollect that when you tell us of certain laws, and customs, and moral evils, and gross crimes, which are often incidents of slavery in this country, we agree with you, and are most anxious for their removal." (*First Letter to Dr.* WAYLAND.)

I have shown in the first chapter of this work, that the definition of slavery, quoted from Paley, and relied on by Dr. Fuller, here, amounts to nothing. It is no more a definition of slavery than a straight line is a definition of a triangle. But even admitting that this is a correct view of slavery, the case is not materially altered; for the service claimed is at war with the original and inalienable rights of mankind — it is a service without the contract or consent of the servant, and we maintain that the Bible never authorized such a relation between man and man.

The effect of this kind of reasoning is to divest

slavery of intrinsic evil — to show that it is not a sin
per se, and may be tolerated if well used.   It is made
to take rank with good things, such as marriage, civil
government, and the parental relation — all which
may be sources of evil, but are essentially right, or at
least not essentially wrong, in themselves.   Hence,
an attempt has been made to make the character of
slavery turn wholly upon the motives of the slave-
holder.

Dr. Bond, who declares himself the staunch enemy
of slavery, takes a position coincident with that assumed by Dr. Fuller, in the foregoing extract :

" Now, when we admitted that slavery was sinful, we spoke
of it as our Discipline does, as systematized in the slave laws
of our Southern States.   In these, slavery is no longer an abstract idea.   It receives body and form, and is actually a wrong
and an outrage on humanity.   We deal in no abstractions.
We look at the thing as it exists, and as it exhibits itself in
its actual operation.   We have not said that slavery as an abstract idea is a sin ; but that slavery, as established by law in
this country, is sinful — a national sin, for which God will inflict national punishment.

" But we further admit, that whoever avails himself of the
power which these laws give him, to hold his fellow man as
property, for gain — not from mercy or benevolence to the
slave — is a sinner before God.   But the quality of the act
depends upon the motive.   It is not the abstract idea of slavery
that characterizes slave-holding, but the motives which influence
the slave-holder, and of these God only can judge.   Men may
hypocritically allege merciful motives for holding slaves, but
men may also urge them sincerely and truly.   No church ju-
dicatory can decide upon motives, when the circumstances of

the case do not make the motives apparent; and therefore no general rule can be applied without wrong and injustice." (*Chris. Adv. and Jour., Nov.* 10, 1852.)

If the character of slavery depends upon the motive, when the motive is good, of course slavery is good. This conclusion is unavoidable, from the above premises. But the doctrine of motives has a wide application — it is not merely the motive of mercy that is allowable, in reference to things in themselves harmless. Gain is a lawful, and even a commendable motive, and one of the principal motives of all industry. And if slavery is neither good nor bad in itself, and its character is wholly determined by motives, it follows that the motive of gain, which is good in itself, may possibly be applied to slavery as well as to other things. It is true that there are acts which demand a higher motive, and if it can be shown that converting our fellow men into chattels personal is one of those high and holy duties from which all secular motives should be excluded, we admit that slave-holding for gain is sinful. The sole motive of slavery is gain. For gain, the negroes were brought to this country, and for gain, they have been kept in bondage up to this hour. No other motive can be alleged, or need to be alleged; the motive is good enough, but the act is wicked, and would be if the motives were ever so exalted. It is not better motives but better acts that the slave-holder needs.

The argument, then, is on the essential nature of slavery, and not on any of its alleged accidents or abuses. If slavery is not a sin, *per se*, it may undoubtedly be so managed as not to become sinful. But if sin is woven into its very nature, or, in other words, if it properly belongs to the class of crimes, then no possible circumstances can justify it. Crime never loses its character. It may be palliated, but cannot be justified — for in that case, it would not be crime. Murder is always murder; theft is always theft, and adultery always adultery. There may be circumstances under which killing a human being, taking property not our own, and sexual intercourse, are lawful; but no one thinks of applying to these acts, when lawful, those names which designate crime. Though killing is not always murder, yet murder itself is always murder. That slavery is often wicked, is conceded. The question now is, whether there can be any force of circumstances or excellence of motives that shall divest slavery of its criminal character. Has slavery the stability and unchangeableness of other crimes, or is its sinfulness only incidental? We affirm that its wickedness is innate and inseparable.

1. It is without a reason. In all cases where particular acts, as, for instance, killing a man, are deemed innocent, they are so deemed for good and sufficient reasons. It must be shown that the killing had not in it the elements of murder — that it was done in self-defence, or in sudden passion, or by accident. So of the taking of property not our own: if it can be made to appear that there was an uncontrollable necessity for such an appropriation of another's goods, and that no felonious purpose was indulged in, the case is only one of trespass and not of theft. Now,

if the advocates of slavery could show any similar reason for the institution, we might regard it as innocent. Could they show that negroes cannot be governed like other men, or that they must be held as chattels, or that they are incapable of " consent and contract" in relation to service — then slavery would stand acquitted. But this they do not attempt, because they know that nothing of the kind exists. They know that slavery is a wanton exercise of power, and that there is not the least necessity for it.

2. It is without right. The boundary which separates sin and holiness, is that which separates good and evil. The form of virtue, or good rules, may sometimes be set aside without injury where constitutional principles are not infracted. Murder is always murder, because it is always wrong — it is always an outrage on the constitutional right to life. The slave has a natural right to be free, and the taking away of this right must be a sin. It is an irreparable loss to the slave, and such a loss as no man has a right to inflict. There is no compensation in the case. It is not a mere *quasi* wrong, nor is it a substitution of one right for another — it is the deliberate crushing of a man into a brute. It is the total extinction of right without any reason, either pretended or real. The slave being by accident of law within the power of the master, is kept within that power, not from any necessity, but simply from the master's choice.

3. Dr. Fuller has given us his idea of what is necessary to free slavery from its turpitude, and restore the institution to pristine purity. But he fails en-

tirely in showing that the institution in its most improved form has either justice or propriety. He shows that it might be less wicked than it is — a truth none will dispute — but he leaves the question of its being wicked at all, wholly out of sight. The sin of murder might be enhanced by circumstances of cruelty, and so may that of slavery ; yet, apart from incidental aggravations of this kind, both acts are criminal. It is the criminality lying back of these alleged abuses that needs an apology, but never finds it. We do not dispute that killing twenty men is a greater sin than killing one man, but the latter act is just as truly murder as if it had been impossible to kill many instead of one. The first step in slavery is a crime, and no array of circumstances can ever make it innocent. We must not overlook an intrinsic evil, because there are extrinsic evils connected with it ; and no amendment of the latter can at all affect the former.

" Wanton cruelty may be too often practiced by masters, as it is by parents ; but this, which is but an occasional incident of slavery, should not be exhibited as the prominent evil. This may be removed by the influence of humane feelings, and especially by Christian principle, but countless evils will still remain, inherent and inseparable from the system." (*Slavery and the Domestic Slave Trade in the United States, by Prof.* E. A. ANDREWS, *p.* 35.)

We are not concerned with the abuses of slavery, but with slavery itself, which is one of the greatest of abuses. It is admitted that murder, robbery and adultery may be accompanied by circumstances of additional atrocity and guilt, yet these circumstances, when wanting, never excuse the original crime. We do not acquit the murderer, because he did not mangle his victim, or the robber, because he did not take all the man possessed, or the adulterer, because he used neither violence nor artifice. The crime is in the act itself, and not in its adjuncts or circumstances; and while the act remains, the sin must remain also.

4. If slavery be not a sin, *per se*, then it follows that the rights of man are not inherent and inalienable. On this supposition, the right to " life, liberty, and the pursuit of happiness," is only a conventional regulation, dependent upon the accident of legislation, and removable at any time without guilt. On this hypothesis, to make a man — any man — a chattel, is no invasion of his personal or civil rights; he may be thrown into market, or into prison, by the mere wantonness of power, and yet no injury is done — he has lost no rights, for he had none to lose. But can anybody believe that man has no natural rights ?—that he is as destitute of such rights as a stock or a stone? Is not the whole frame-work of civil law declarative of natural rights existing in man as man, and is it not confessedly the whole object of such law to protect these rights? To this question there can be but one answer: all know that law is a farce and a usurpation, unless it aims to promote the public welfare by carefully guarding the rights of individuals. It follows, therefore, that slavery is wrong under all circumstances, or right under all circumstances. If wrong is

possible, then is slavery wrong; but if not possible, then slavery is guiltless. If man has rights to lose, slavery takes them away; but if he has none, of course, none are·taken away.

5. If slavery may be justified by circumstances, then vice and virtue are not immutable in their natures; they are only accidents of things, which may or may not belong to them. This supposes that man may exist without obligations or rights; that he may have neither duties to perform, nor privileges to enjoy. It supposes, in fact, that man can, at the same time, be man and not man, which is a glaring contradiction. We cannot limit the doctrine, that slavery is not an intrinsic moral evil, to slavery alone; for if true of this, it is equally true of other things. It applies to all other men, and makes the invasion of their rights a matter of indifference; they, having the same human nature as the slave, can have no rights superior to his. But we must go one step further. If rights are out of the question here, then are they everywhere. Natural and personal rights fall not alone. The whole superstructure of morals is destroyed. Our duties to God and man cease to be duties, and there is no obligation of any kind whatever, except that of mere physical force. Let it be affirmed that slavery is not a sin, *per se*, and it follows inevitably that there is no sin. A more glaring violation of right than slavery, there cannot be; and we are compelled to deny the existence of moral evil, or acknowledge that slavery is one of the highest crimes.

6. There is another class of apologies, almost too

futile to be noticed. These are based on the pre-existence of the evil, and on the supremacy of the State. It is enough to say of all such defences, that they will apply just as well to idolatry or murder. It is no justification of crime that it has long been tolerated; otherwise, the attempt to reform man from inveterate crimes would be an absurdity. Nor is it of more consequence that the State countenances or requires the commission of wrongs. In other cases, we never think of pleading such authority for things acknowledged to be sinful. No man — no Christian man — would deem the requisition of civil government a sufficient excuse for worshiping an idol. The whole argument in this direction is too superficial to bear a moment's investigation. States or governments have no right to enslave men, and what they have not a right to do themselves, they cannot authorize individuals to do. But still we are told, " it is not a sin under the circumstances." What these circumstances are, that transmute crime into virtue, has been abundantly shown, and we have also shown that they are no justification at all. The State throws embarrassments in the way of emancipation, therefore slavery is no crime! Suppose we change the terms of this enthymeme a little : the State throws embarrassments in the way of chastity, therefore adultery is no crime. Will the objector admit this ? If not, let him confess at once that circumstances cannot change vice into virtue. He may take which position he chooses, either that slavery is a crime, or that it is not a crime; but he cannot be allowed both — he must not vault from one to the other, as this destroys the meaning of language, and confounds all moral distinctions. Murder is murder, and theft is theft, under all circumstances; and so of the crime of slavery — if a crime at all, it is always a crime. If the State were to hold out the strongest inducements to drunkenness and dishonesty — nay, if it were to enjoin the commission of these crimes, and back the injunction with the heaviest penalties — with disfranchisement, confiscation, and death — would it be right for us to comply? Would it change, in any respect, the character of these sins? By no means. That the State practically forbids emancipation, and thereby enjoins a continual robbery of the colored man's rights, is beyond dispute. But it is just as much beyond dispute in this case as in the former, that the difficulties thrown in the way do not render innocent the slave-holding which they are intended to perpetuate. It is just as much a sin to hold a slave, as it would be if the State had done nothing to promote slavery. The essential rights of the colored man are born with him; they do not depend upon the State; he does not acquire them by legislation, nor can they be legislated away from him. For this reason, it will always be a crime to strip him of those rights, no matter what he may gain or lose by their possession; they are his as inalienably as the blood in his veins, or the breath in his lungs.

CHAPTER V.

SLAVERY NOT SANCTIONED BY THE OLD TESTAMENT.

MUCH stress has been laid on the authority of the Scriptures, especially the Old Testament, by the supporters of slavery. They appear to think that the system finds an impregnable defense in the Word of God. Their appeal to the Bible, however, is most unfortunate for their cause, as no other book in the world is so decidedly hostile to oppression, and wrongdoing of every kind. But still, as they have chosen this arbitrament, they should have whatever advantage it may afford. If it can possibly be shown that a book, which teaches all right to be done to all men, does, nevertheless, sanction slavery, slave-holders are justly entitled to the benefit of such showing, and very much need it.

It should be understood in the outset, that the Old Testament is not, in all respects, a standard of morals for the present day. The New Testament has revised the ethical code of the Old, and several things, once allowed, are now prohibited. As instances of the kind, we mention, 1. Wars, both offensive and defensive; 2. Polygamy; 3. Concubinage; 4. Putting children to death; 5. Bills of divorce; 6. Slaying of murderers by their relatives. These practices, however tolerated in Patriarchal and Jewish times, are manifestly contrary to both the spirit and the letter

of the Gospel.   Hence, it does not by any means follow, as a necessary consequence, that the recognition
of slavery, by Moses, gives it a place among the institutions of Christianity.

Servitude was tolerated and regulated by law under the Mosaic institute ; but servitude is not slavery.
There is a wide difference between any form of mere
servitude, and slavery. The servant may have the
rights of a man in several respects; he may own
property, have wife and children, and be regarded as
a man.   But the slave can own nothing, acquire
nothing, and be nothing, before the law, but a chattel.   It is further to be conceded, that servants were
bought and sold by the Jews; yet it does not appear
that such servants were regarded as chattels personal,
or that the traffic in this species of property was ever
extensive.   Further than this, no concession can be
made.   The first, and most important element of
slavery — that of entire subjection to the master —
did not exist among them.   No Hebrew was permitted to usurp the place of God.   Servants there were,
but no slaves.   I shall here set down some of the circumstances which distinguished servitude as it prevailed among the Israelites, and which made slavery,
in the proper sense of the word, an utter impossibility.

1. Their government was a Theocracy.   God was
supreme governor.   Hence, no man could at any time
claim to rule according to his own will.   Under such
a system of laws, the rights of conscience are always

protected. But it is far otherwise where the Higher Law is scouted, and the will of man is made the only rule of duty. Slavery was excluded from the Jewish polity by this feature of its constitution, as effectually as it could have been by a specific enactment.

2. The whole scope of the Mosaic institute was in opposition to the inequality and degradation peculiar to slavery. The law of BROTHERHOOD prevailed everywhere, uprooting and destroying that aristocratic pride, which is the foundation of slavery. The people were taught to respect man, and to recognize in every man a brother. Depressed he might be, but he was not to be cast from the pale of humanity. Not so with slavery. The slave is reduced to the condition of a brute, and the law makes no provision for his elevation to the rank from which he has been degraded. The Jew saw in his servant a brother, for whom he was in duty bound to provide, and who was to be, with him, a sharer of immortality. His servant was, equally with himself, a creature of God, and entitled to every kindness.

3. The Jewish polity was a system of mercy. Its humanizing influence was felt in a thousand ways, on both masters and servants. It taught men to live for eternity, and not for time. It inspired hopes of a better inheritance, where the vices and ills of this world should be unknown. Every Jew, properly instructed, was spiritual, and held all his worldly possessions as a tenant at will of the Most High. It was his duty to perfect holiness in the fear of God. His religion, if fully carried out, cut off all sinful indul-

gences, and prevented all oppression. It was based on the law of love, as well as on the law of purity. "Thou shalt love thy neighbor as thyself." (*Lev.* xix: 18.)

4. All servants were to be taught the principles of religion, and admitted to all the rights and privileges of divine worship. The master was specially charged to bring his servants with him when he appeared before the Lord. (*See Gen.* xvii: 12, *and Deut.* xvi: 9–14.)

5. In the year of jubilee all servants were to go free. This applied, not only to servants of the Hebrew stock, but to all others. "Ye shall hallow the year, and proclaim liberty throughout all the land, to all the inhabitants thereof." (*Lev.* xxv: 10.)

6. Servants were permitted to live together in families, and their domestic relations were held sacred. (*See Lev.* xix: 20.)

7. The servant who was abused by his master, was to be set free. (*See Exod.* xxi: 26, 27.)

8. The master who violated the chastity of his female servant, was obliged to marry her, or let her go free. (*See Exod.* xxi: 8–11, *Deut.* xxi: 10–14.)

9. The servant who escaped from his master, was not to be delivered up. This regulation alone was sufficient to protect the servant from everything analogous to slavery. This is understood by some as applying only to those servants who escaped from the surrounding idolatrous nations, and sought a refuge among the Jews. But there is nothing in the passage itself, nor in the context, that favors such a construc-

tion. It is a meaning brought to the text, and not one deduced from it. The words are plain :

" Thou shalt not deliver unto his master the servant which is escaped from his master unto thee : he shall dwell with thee, even among you, in that place which he shall choose in one of thy gates, where it liketh him best: thou shalt not oppress him." (*Deut.* xxiii : 15, 16.)

It is said that this must be restricted to servants from foreign nations, because it would be unjust if applied to Hebrew servants. Such an objection to a liberal construction of the text, is disrespectful — it gives the Israelite permission to wrong the foreigner, by keeping his servant, and obliges him to deal fairly only with his own countrymen. If there was injustice in not restoring the servant of the Hebrew, there was equal injustice in not restoring the servant of one belonging to a neighboring tribe. But the truth is, the servant, belong to whom he might, was not to be given up. When so oppressed that conscience and safety demanded flight, he was permitted to flee, and thus escape a tyranny that would have crushed his manhood. This compelled masters to treat servants well, and secure the continuance of their services by kindness, rather than by force. It placed masters and servants on much the same terms that prevail in free countries, where labor is hired. The employer must pay well, and demean himself correctly, or his help will leave him. He is not, in any case, the owner of the men, but the buyer of their services, and the relation may be dissolved when it is deemed necessary by either party. So, we think, the Israelitish servant, whom the master was bound to love as himself, had the privilege of going free, when conscience and honor demanded it. That the servant from another nation was to be accorded this right, none can dispute ; and that the right might be equally important to the servant of a Hebrew, is as little questionable. Under this regulation, oppression could reach only a certain extent. Masters were dependent upon their good behavior for the retention of their servants, as all masters ought to be. Men might sell their services, and the services of their children, as thousands prefer to do in all countries ; but the law would not allow the contract to run always — it must expire at the year of jubilee. And, even while the obligation of service remained, it was to be forfeited by specific acts of abuse, and might be terminated at the discretion of the servant. In short, provision was made for humanity. The master could not oblige his servant to violate God's law, nor to become a brute. The servant was to be a WILLING servant. Nothing like constraint is authorized, and all oppression is strictly forbidden. Those who chose servitude could only remain servants upon the ignominious condition of having their ears bored through with an awl.

Let those who object to the view we have taken of the foregoing passage, consider —

1. That the spirit and letter of the Old Testament were vastly elevated above the institutions of paganism, and that it is therefore safer to follow the upward tendency of the former, than it is the downward analogies of the latter. Heathenism would not have

allowed the servant to escape; neither would it have afforded a jubilee, in which he might go out without an escape. A system which provided for the release of all, at a stated time, may be supposed to have admitted of the release of the oppressed at any time.

2. That servitude, like divorce or polygamy, was not a part of the Mosaic religion, but an evil, tolerated under an imperfect dispensation, and because the hearts of the people were hard. Hence, all regulations on the subject are to be construed against servitude, and not in favor of it. The bill of divorce was allowed, but it was not intended to promote the separation of man and wife; so the holding of servants was permitted, but it was not designed to make bondage an unconditional and interminable state.

3. That to afford protection to fugitives from other masters, and not to those from Jewish masters, was most unequal; giving to the foreigner a privilege denied to the Jew: whereas, there is abundant evidence that the Israelitish servant was to be treated with special tenderness.

4. That the Jews were all fugitives when these precepts were delivered — having fled from Egyptian servitude; and that rules made for such a people, on the treatment of fugitives, would naturally be of the most comprehensive character. There was, as yet, no servants among them — their laws were only prospective — and it may well be supposed, that He who led a nation of bondmen to liberty, would teach them to be the protectors of all other bondmen, and especially those of their own country.

5. That the exodus of the Israelites was in fact nothing but an assumption of this very right to go forth and be free, at their own option, when compelled by the obligations of duty. This great national act of self-emancipation was to constitute an example for all the oppressed. In no other way could man be man, when the voice of duty called.

6. That the Jew was always required to remember that he had been a bondman, and this for the avowed purpose of softening his treatment toward those in his service. We may safely conclude, also, that this remembrance was intended to prepare him to accord to his servants the same right to escape, which himself had enjoyed in so marvelous a manner.

Now, we contend that the advocates of slavery, if they mean to avail themselves of the Old Testament, must use its authority in support of such a system as we have here described. But this system has scarcely any resemblance to American Slavery. The argument, therefore, is entirely worthless. Even if the servitude provided for by the laws of Moses had not been canceled by a new and better dispensation, it could have afforded no countenance to the diabolical system of slavery established in this country. But should we concede all, the argument could do them no good. It would be just as conclusive to adduce the Mosaic law in favor of polygamy, in order to justify a plurality of wives, as it is to adduce it in support of any type of slavery. If the authority is good in one case, it is in another. Nor do we by this weaken the authority of such parts of the Mosaic code as have not been repealed. What has been confirmed by Christ, and adopted into the New Testament, is obligatory; but all the rest is annulled. The law of circumcision, though vital to the Jew, is not binding upon us. And so of the whole Jewish ritual, and all the other laws not strictly of a moral character.

CHAPTER VI.

SLAVERY NOT SANCTIONED BY THE NEW TESTAMENT.

WE must abide the teaching of the New Testament. If its authority is clearly on the side of slavery, then slavery — whatever we may think of it — ought to be tolerated in the Church. If He whose kingdom was not of this world — who came not to destroy men's lives, but to save them — and who commanded his disciples to love one another as he had loved them, did, nevertheless, sanction chattel slavery with all its horrors, then we must bow to the mandate, and place it among the most inscrutable mysteries of Divine Providence. We know not as any serious attempt has been made to press the words of Christ into the support of slavery. It would be difficult to find a single text in the Evangelists that could with decency be used for such a purpose. Slavery does not appear to have flourished in Judea at the time of the Advent, and consequently the personal ministry of Christ afforded few or no opportunities for discussing the subject. It was not his practice to introduce foreign vices for animadversion and reproof. He laid down rules for all virtue, and interdicted all sin, but confined the illustration and application of his precepts chiefly to things under his immediate, personal observation. We shall, therefore, find the argument resting mainly on some expressions in the apostolic Epistles. The apostles went abroad, and saw slavery in all its forms; they wrote to Churches living where slavery abounded, and if the system was worthy of adoption, or countenance, or condemnation, we may reasonably expect to find it so treated in their letters. In this expectation we are not disappointed. The references to servitude are few, but exceedingly clear. The following passage may be taken as an instance:

"Art thou called being a servant? care not for it; but if thou mayest be made free, use it rather. For he that is called in the Lord, being a servant, is the Lord's free man: likewise, also, he that is called, being free, is Christ's servant. Ye are bought with a price; be not ye the servants of men." (1. *Cor.* vii, 21–23.)

This shows that Christianity utterly annihilates the slave system — the servant is so far made free by his conversion, that he may look upon all that remains of bondage as of no importance, and "care not for it." He is CHRIST'S FREE MAN, and is forbidden to be the servant of men. That is, he is free to obey Christ in all things, and not permitted to serve men in any thing contrary to the law of Christ. The course of the apostle's argument here shows that we have not misapprehended nor overstated the matter. He was teaching the Corinthians to abide as they were called: the circumcised in their circumcision, and the uncircumcised in their uncircumcision; the married as married, and the unmarried as unmarried. He would have them understand that the gospel did not depend for its efficiency on any of these external things, and that by their translation into the kingdom of God, they had gained a position which enabled them to look down upon all worldly circumstances with comparative indifference. The servant of man had become not only a servant, but "an heir of God, and joint heir with Christ." One elevated to such immortal honors and immunities, if claimed as the slave of man, might well "care not for it." It could do him no harm, because he was so fully brought under a higher law, and into the protection of a greater Sovereign, that all human authority was paralyzed, except in things lawful to be done.

There is another passage which, if possible, shows still more plainly this independence of the converted servant.

"Servants, be obedient to them that are your masters according to the flesh, with fear and trembling, in singleness of your heart, as unto Christ. Not with eye service, as menpleasers; but as the servants of Christ, doing the will of God from the heart; with good will doing service, as to the Lord, and not to men: knowing that whatsoever good thing any man doeth, the same shall he receive of the Lord, whether he be bond or free." (*Eph.*, vi, 5–8.)

Here the human master's authority is completely absorbed, so to speak, in the will of God. The servant is not allowed to consider himself the servant of man, but the servant of God. "As THE SERVANTS OF CHRIST, DOING THE WILL OF GOD FROM THE HEART" this is obviously not a rule for a chattel personal — a thing; but for a man in the highest state of religious and moral freedom. No service incompatible with the holiness of God, was to be tolerated. The man was to reckon himself as doing service only to Christ— thus implying that he sustained an infinitely higher relation than to man, and was under supreme obligation, not to his master, but to his master's Master. Both servant and master were made to feel that they equally had a Master, who was God, and to whom they must give account for all their deeds. There could be no substitution in the case; one could not answer for another — each must do right or perish. God was before them, and his law was the only law of both master and servant. Such precepts leave no room for slavery, unless slavery is holy; it must be as pure as God, or it cannot have the slightest authority. The servant has to do every moment with the law of one who forbids sin, and if all the men in the universe were to command him to sin, he ought to spurn their authority and obey his God. But waiving further comment on particular passages, we shall present a few general observations, which will furnish the reader with a wider view of the subject. If slavery was incorporated with Christianity by Christ, or his apostles, the question is settled — we have no right to innovate. But if they rejected it, we ought to do the same — if they brought it into the Church, we have no right to expel it.

That the apostles did not admit slavery or slaveholders into the Church, is evident to us, from the following considerations:

1. They did not, because they could not. The nature and constitution of the Church would not admit of it. In the first place, slavery is a civil institution, but the Church is a spiritual institution, and could not incorporate this element of the civil law. If there was slavery in the Church, it must have been spiritual slavery, for the Church had no civil code by which to uphold slavery. In the next place, the Church is holy, but slavery is unholy, therefore, it could not come into the Church by apostolic sanction.

2. All the apostolic letters were addressed to spiritual communities — "holy brethren," whose rule of living was universal righteousness, and whose members were all equally free in Christ, and on a level with each other — each and all standing by faith, and by faith only. To reach this point, where "all are one," and to be a member of the "communion of saints," for whom the apostles wrote, it was necessary to renounce every worldly and social distinction, for in Christ there could be "neither Jew nor Greek, neither bond nor free, neither male nor female." Those who think the apostles introduced chattel slavery into this sublime brotherhood, must have a taste for the marvelous. We could as soon believe that Mahomet made a journey to heaven on the beast Alborak.

3. A slave, be it remembered, " is a person who is wholly subject to the will of another" human being. But no Christian can be thus bound. Hence, the slave-law must of necessity be a dead letter wherever Christianity prevails. For all Christians acknowledge God as their Master. If the slave-holder could get into the Church, his entrance there would strip him of every particle of that unrighteous authority with which the civil law had invested him. In the world, men can hold slaves, but not in Christ — not in the Church. The apostles did not write for the world, but for the Church, and hence they gave no directions for slave-holding.

4. The duties enjoined on believers are wholly incompatible with slavery. " Let each esteem other better than themselves" — that is, the master esteem the slave better than himself. " In honor preferring one another" — that is, the master counting his slave more honorable than himself, and conceding to him, on all occasions, the place of honor. "Therefore, all things whatsoever ye would that men should do unto you, do ye even so unto them" — that is, if you, being a slave, would prefer liberty, grant it to your slaves. Now who does not see that these precepts effectually annihilate the system of slavery? And yet no man can be a Christian without obeying all these commands, and many others equally at variance with the slave-law — a law which is nothing better with us than it was with the old Romans, who held their slaves "*pro nullis, pro mortuis, pro quadrupedibus*" — " as nothing, as dead, as quadrupeds." No wonder that

the Saviour and his apostles, after giving such precepts, did not give directions for the emancipation of slaves. It would have been just as absurd in them to do so, as it would, after commanding parents to "bring up their children in the nurture and admonition of the Lord," to add a precept against infanticide.

5. The injunctions given to masters and servants, (*Eph.* vi, 5–9, and elsewhere,) neither afford countenance to slavery, nor proof that slave-holding was introduced into the Church, under any modification. It is true, the words *doulos* and *kurios* are used, and if we can make one mean a chattel slave, we can make the other mean God. One of these terms is often applied to slaves, and the other quite as often applied to Christ. But who does not know that in the Scriptures words often acquire a new and very different meaning. If we adhere to the literal and classical use of terms, we shall land not only in slavery, but in popery, and even in Manicheism. The Papist renders τουτο εστι το σωμα μου — "this is my body," literally, and makes out transubstantiation. When the apostle says, "I know that in me, (that is, in my flesh,) dwelléth no good thing," we have only to adhere to this excessive literalism to reach the Manichean notion, that all evil resides in matter. If we choose to be as absurd in our interpretation, and make the apostle use terms precisely as a heathen would have used them, we may possibly make him an authority for slave-holding. The fact that commands are given to servants and masters to discharge faithfully their respective duties, does by no means prove that these servants and mas-

ters stood to each other in the relation of slaves and slave-owners. This would be to suppose that a wicked civil institution of idolatrous heathen, was adopted into the holy, spiritual Church of the true God. A supposition so monstrous and improbable, that we can scarcely conceive how it ever entered the mind of any man having the slightest acquaintance with Christianity. Servants there might be, masters there might be, but the men who sustained these relations in the Church were " new creatures ;" old things had passed away, and both master and servant had come under a new law, to which chattel-slavery was unknown — the law of justice and equality, the law of love and brotherly kindness.

6. If slavery was introduced into the Church by the apostles, it was introduced with all its attributes, its buying and selling, its whipping and killing, its lust and degradation. The institution was transplanted entire, if at all, except so far as it might be regulated by the few directions given to servants and masters. This would have left Paul at liberty to purchase or sell any of his brethren who were slaves — it left the whole Church open to the slave traffic, for there is not one word said in the apostolic Epistles against buying men, women and children, with an intention to enslave them. We leave the candid to judge whether it is likely that so radical a reform as Christianity would participate in such a vile business. Indeed, it seems to us that were the Scriptures much more susceptible of being perverted to the support of slavery than they are, both the head and the heart of every

Christian must instantly repel the enormity, and stamp all pro-slavery renderings as utterly spurious.

7. The most that can be made of the apostle's doctrine and practice is, that he exhorted those who had servants to treat them well, and those who were servants, to be faithful to their masters — duties which, to say the least, are quite as applicable to non-slave-holders as to slave-holders, and to freemen as to slaves. And we can see no reason for the sweeping inference, that the apostle had, contrary to the spirit of the Gospel which he preached, introduced into the Church the horrible, blood-stained system of chattel slavery — a system every way as uncongenial with Christianity as idolatry itself. The language employed on this subject carries with it internal evidence that these were hired servants: "Masters, give unto your servants that which is just and equal." This is not a manner of speaking known to the slave code.

8. But slavery and slave-holding in the Church are impossible, because Christianity is conservative of human rights. The master may rob his fellow man of liberty, and get the law of man to sanction the foul deed, but he cannot be accommodated in this way by the law of God. On entering the Church, he must himself become a servant. Here the unrighteous grasp of human power must yield to a higher authority. Men cannot carry a slave even into the kingdom of Great Britain, for the moment a slave sets foot on British soil, he is as free as his master ; and how much less can they bring a slave into the kingdom of God!

CHAPTER VII.

SLAVERY NEVER AN ACT OF BENEVOLENCE.

ONE of the most specious, but futile, arguments in favor of slavery, is derived from its supposed benevolence under certain circumstances. Men who acknowledge the institution to be wicked, still insist that it ought to be tolerated as an act of mercy to the slave. In their estimation, to obey a wicked law is not necessarily a crime, " because the relation between master and slave may be such that the law of love itself may forbid emancipation." (Dr. BOND, *Chris. Adv. and Jour.*, *Aug.* 18, 1852.) This is sheer assumption. There is no possibility that any such relation should exist. If this assumption be admitted, the argument is at an end, for the law of love must be kept; but the admission is impossible, and for the following reasons:

1. If the law of love forbids emancipation, it becomes, in so far, identical with the slave law, which is an evil law — hence, one of these two things must result, either the law of love becomes evil, or the evil law of slavery becomes good. But neither of these things can ever happen, and consequently the law of love can never forbid emancipation.

2. If the law of love enjoins slavery as a preventive of greater evil, then it follows that a Christian is bound to do some evil in order to keep wicked men

from doing more evil. He must hold a slave — that
is, reduce a man to a chattel — lest other men should
not only reduce the man to a chattel, but heap upon
him additional injuries, such as cruelty, separation
from his family, and so forth. On this principle, if
the law should require the master to put out his slave's
eyes, under a threat that if he did not comply, the
slave's eyes should not only be put out by somebody
else, but his hands and feet should be cut off, — the
master would be bound to obey! The same principle
would oblige us to kill one man — to commit one
murder — in order to prevent ten other murders being
committed. But no Christian can admit such a horrible obligation, and, consequently, no Christian can
admit that he is obliged to deprive a man of some of
his rights, in order to keep the man from greater
wrongs.

3. The slave law, being essentially evil, can never
produce good. The heavenly fruit of brotherly kindness never grows on such a satanic root of bitterness.
" Do men gather grapes of thorns, or figs of thistles ?"
To keep the slave law, even in its best form, is to be
cruel and unjust, because it takes away God-given
rights — but it may not be to reach the utmost depths
of cruelty and injustice. Some forms of piracy are
worse than others, but does it therefore follow that
any form of piracy is tolerable? If there is kindness
in robbing a man of a thousand dollars, in order to
prevent his being robbed of ten thousand, it is such
kindness as no honest man can show. It is a kindness which God has forbidden, and which none but

wicked men and devils should ever dare to practice.
Yet, this is the boasted law of love, as it obtains between the slave and the master — the latter robs, but
takes not everything, as some fiercer robber might do.

4. The relation between master and slave is the
same as between any other two men. There is no
different code of ethics for the adjustment of this relation — no rules of duty applicable here, and not
elsewhere. Men, standing in this relation, have all
the rights and immunities belonging to other men —
nothing more, nothing less. The direction to masters
is, to "give to their servants that which is just and
equal;" not what is just and equal according to the
slave law, but what is just and equal between man
and man — between brethren, children of the same
Heavenly Father. There is nothing in this relation
to make it necessary to keep up the relation. The
slave may suffer more, if he be not still enslaved by
his former master, but this, as we have shown, does
not authorize that master to take away any portion of
his rights. He may not obey a wicked law, and deprive a man of his liberty, for fear some one else
should take advantage of the same law, and deprive
the man of still more.

5. Such an operation of the law of love would be
contrary to the genius of Christianity. Restoration
is the doctrine of religion. When Zaccheus was converted, he did not propose to retain the property that
he had taken wrongfully from others, and use it faithfully for their good, but he promised to restore it, and
even more, to the original owners. Now, the slave

has been robbed of his liberty, and the master is bound to make restitution. Had the robbery consisted in taking money, all will see that Christianity would demand the restoration of the money, as far as possible, on the part of the repentant transgressor. But where the offence consists in taking what is infinitely more valuable than money — in stealing the man himself, how much more evident is it that the man should be restored to himself!

6. In another important particular, this modified slave-holding is at war with the gospel. It is not the way to produce reform. The wicked institutions of society are to be renounced. Slavery being a grievous wrong, the Christian is not to participate in it, under the delusive impression that he shall thereby reform the institution. He might, on the same principle, continue gambling and horse-racing, with the hope of introducing more humanity into those corrupt practices.

7. It is said that the slave, if liberated, will be snatched by the slave-trader, and doomed to bondage. And is he not already in bondage? what has he more to dread? and what good does the law of love confer on him by forbidding his emancipation? Nor are we clear that the danger of a re-enslavement is not altogether exaggerated. There are thousands of free blacks in all the slave States, and we have yet to learn that slave-holders, generally, are so abominably wanting in common honesty as to try to enslave free colored men. The pretence of keeping the slave in bonds, in order to keep him from the clutches of the

slave-trader, is a miserable fallacy — nay, horrid mockery of the sacred virtue of kindness. It is like shooting a man through the heart, to save his life. It is plundering a man of all he has, even to his manhood, for the sole purpose of saving him from robbery! Oh shame, where is thy blush! This foul, total robbery — this unexampled and unmeasured thieving, is perpetrated in the name of justice and mercy. It is just as much worse than common robbery, as it is more extensive in degree, and more false in character. There is no need of any man's falling into the hands of a slave-trader, unless he is a slave — a freeman can always keep clear of those desperadoes; but a slave must follow the laws of property, and be sold at auction, or private sale, whenever the master chooses, and to whomsoever he chooses. In case of insolvency, he must be sold, like any other property, to the highest bidder. Such an one may be caught up by the slave-dealer, but not the man who has free papers in his pocket — who is liable for no master's debts, and, withal, is on his way, post haste, to the land of the free. Throwing a man into the crater of a volcano, to guard him against spontaneous combustion; or, into the depths of the ocean, to keep him from the pattering rain-drops of a summer shower, would be wisdom and mercy, compared with slave-holding as a remedy for the evils of emancipation.

8. If the law forbids emancipation, it forbids our "ceasing to do evil." For the law which binds the slave is admitted to be "evil, only evil, and that continually." To keep the slave bound, this evil law

must be kept in force against him, and we must continue to do evil, notwithstanding the express command of God to the contrary. Thus does this absurd attempt to make the law of love subservient to slaveholding, not only array us in open hostility to heaven, but it makes us miserable tools of the most depraved human legislation.

9. Again, if the law of love forbids emancipation, it sanctions the perpetual degradation of the slave, in opposition to all the elevating tendencies of the gospel. It is the design of religion to banish all unrighteousness and tyranny from the earth, but this coalescence of the Church with slave-holding stops the work of reform, and converts the means of freedom into an engine of oppression. And wherefore? Why, simply to mitigate the sufferings of the slave for a time. This may be an opiate, but it is not a remedy. And it is a very costly opiate. To eternize the evil for the sake of lessening it in some degree, is a foolish bargain — such as neither love nor wisdom can ever make.

10. But then nothing permanent is gained. The Christian slave-master may backslide, or become bankrupt, or die, and in either case what security has the slave of continued good treatment? In a moment, all power to keep the slave from the auction block may forever be lost, and love, so far from forbidding emancipation, dictates that the present moment be seized for that purpose — that emancipation be instant, lest the night of death, or of sin, or of misfortune, come and prevent the good work. Love cannot coun-

sel delay, in a matter of justice, especially where, by delay, all hope of justice perishes. And yet, we are gravely told, that, " to require emancipation as a condition of Church fellowship, would be to require men to commit sin — to violate the obligations of humanity and mercy, in order to enter the Church." As well commit sin by ceasing to blaspheme. The liar who speaks the truth, the thief who ceases to steal, and the murderer who ceases to kill, are just as much " violating the obligations of humanity and mercy," as is the man who sets his slaves free. If emancipation is sin, then it is a sin to be honest.

11. To regard slavery as a mercy, is a very foolish assumption. It may be that it is mercy for one man to hold slaves in comparison to what it would be for another to hold them; but this supposes that they must be held as slaves by somebody. It takes for granted that emancipation is impossible. But we deny that emancipation is impossible. The under-ground rail-road is doing too good a business — the odious fugitive slave law has too frequently been had in requisition, to leave any doubt on the public mind as to the practicability of freedom for the slave. It will require a pretty stringent police, to enforce such an act of mercy, as keeping a man and his family chattels forever on one side of the Ohio river, while they might be enjoying liberty on the other side. Of such mercy as this no man would wish to be a partaker. The slave will quickly plant himself in a land of freedom, if the sanctimonious, Judas-like kindness of his master does not prevent him. If the law of love, as

expounded by those who fatten upon the unpaid toil of these sable sons and daughters of Africa, does not prove a mill-stone around the fugitive's neck, to sink him in the sea of despotism, he will be quickly free, in spite of dangers or difficulties. This pious slave-holding is the most horrible of all, because it is so evidently hypocritical. Every body sees it is " stealing the livery of heaven to serve the devil in." We do not dispute that some slave-holders are worse than others, but this does not prove that any are good. No man can hold slaves without doing them wrong. He must deprive them of rights which God has made inalienably theirs, and this deprivation is necessarily a sin. It is this taking away of sacred rights, which gives to the American slave-law its sinful character, and whoever consents to hold a man under this law, is guilty of sanctioning and enforcing the crime which the law ordains. To hold the man as an act of mercy is impossible, except upon the assumed and silly hypothesis, that he must always be a slave.

12. It is supposed that slave-holding must be an act of mercy, because the motives of some who hold slaves are kind. But good motives are no justification of a bad act. One man robs you to get money to pay an honest debt, and one murders you to prevent your injuring another person — the first may be better than a common robber, and the second better than a common murderer, but neither of them has done right ; the one is still a robber, and the other still a murderer. So it is with slave-holders. The man who keeps slaves for gain is probably worse than the man who keeps

them from the mistaken notion of mercy, but both are veritable slave-holders, and guilty of robbing a fellow-being of his God-given rights. Neither of these are fit for Church membership.

It should be understood at once and forever, that slavery is one of those things for which right motives cannot exist. It belongs to the category of crimes, and whatever the motive may be, the act is always bad.

But we are told that " it is not the abstract idea of slavery that characterizes slave-holding." (*Ante, p.* 55.) In this lies one of the fundamental errors of our opponents. They will have it that we should look to the motives of the act in order to determine its moral character. In our judgment, this is just as wise as it would be to look into the motives which lead to other great crimes. Good motives may extenuate the fault, in some degree, but they can never justify it.

They concede that the act is bad when the motive is bad, but in this they have totally overlooked the character of slavery. They might just as well have said that idolatry is bad when the motives are bad. This view makes slavery a good and useful institution, if properly maintained. It is, in short, the high-toned southern view of the subject, combined with that species of denunciation which most southern men exercise towards what they call the evils of slavery. This gives us, we suppose, the sentiments of the advocates of religious slave-holding on this important subject. They are not opposed to slavery, but only to the evils of slavery. They dislike American slavery very much, but, bad as it is, they are anxious that the Church shall still practice it. They would even have no general rule on the subject, because it is so difficult to discriminate between those who hold slaves from good and those who hold them from bad motives. And in this we shall not differ with them — for if bona fide slavery is to be in the Church, it is hardly worth while to discriminate between the motives which inflict the abomination upon us. If crime there must be in the Church, we care little from what source it comes.

13. It is further claimed that the law of love requires slave-holding, in order to prevent the separation of families. It is said that husbands and wives, parents and children, have no other means of remaining together, but to remain in bondage. But it must be borne in mind that husband and wife are terms unknown to the slave code, and unregarded in practice.

Whatever the Church may recognize in the case, slave marriages are not known in law, and consequently, there can be no security for the family compact while the parties remain slaves. So far as the law is concerned, no separation is possible, for no legal union was ever allowed — nothing but promiscuous concubinage. And even this wretched condition the Church is wholly powerless to maintain. The slave is property, and must follow the laws of property, whatever may become of his so-called wife and reputed children. The question now is two-fold; first, whether this precarious relation is worth preserving at the awful price of perpetual bondage; second, whether the separation incident to emancipation will be greater than that incident to slavery. We take the negative of both. It is even doubtful whether the Church has a moral right to marry slaves—she must exact of them promises which they have no power to keep. The husband may be sold the next hour after his marriage, and never see his wife more; how can such a man "comfort, honor, and keep" his wife "in sickness and in health"? And how can the wife "obey, honor, serve, and keep" her husband, in sickness and health, to the end of life? The fact is, the marriage ceremony is profaned, and the Church exacts a lie whenever she repeats it over slaves. She might as well marry cattle. The State intends concubinage, and nothing more—here the Church must rest, and the display of her sacred ceremonies is but solemn mockery. And yet we are told that the "ministers of the Methodist Episcopal Church solemnize these rites as readily among colored as white persons, imposing the same obligations, and exacting the same promises." (*Chris. Adv. and Jour., Nov.* 10, 1852.)

Some separation of families, thus held together, there may be, in consequence of emancipation, but it ends with one generation; whereas, to keep them together, under such circumstances, if it could be done, would entail on all successive generations, the guilt and contingency peculiar to slave families. Slavery renders men incompetent to marriage, and there is no way to throw off the incompetency, but to throw off that which occasions it. If separation were confined to emancipation, the question would be varied, but it is not; and it is our opinion that the domestic slave-trade, the insolvencies, the caprices, the speculations, and the necessities of slave-holders, will produce a thousand times more rending of "marriage obligations and parental ties," than would be produced by sending the slaves to a free State.

It is objected that many of the slaves are not in a condition to be emancipated — infancy, old age, imbecility, and insanity, are the barriers. Would this be a good reason for keeping white men slaves? If not, it is of no force here. Such persons are objects of special kindness, not of brutal degradation and chattelhood. Worse off they could not be — better they might be possibly. These extreme cases, however, are comparatively few in number, and do not affect the general question of emancipation. The slaves, much too commonly for the wishes of their masters, are ready to incur all the expense, danger and separation incident to an escape into a land of freedom. Let it be known that dogs, horses, guns and manacles will not be in requisition to frustrate their attempts, and these men — yes, even the aged and infirm — will quickly bid adieu to the tender mercies of the slave-holder — mercies which, though specious, are, nevertheless, cruel. These difficult cases should never stand alone. They require to be offset by the immense evils which attach to them as they are. If the wretched would suffer as freemen, it must be remembered that they will suffer as slaves. We are told that suffering and injustice must follow emancipation, just as though but for emancipation nothing of the kind would ever happen. Is not slavery all suffering, all injustice? Why, then, insist on the perpetuation of slavery as a preventive of these evils? If slave-holders would do wrong in emancipating their slaves, they must do far greater wrong not to emancipate them. If wrong must be done, let them by all means take that course which will do the least. But the wrongs of emancipation are more fancied than real; they are, for the most part, an idle bugbear, conjured up to relieve the consciences of slave-holders, when pressed by the claims of their unoffending victims. Interest, not humanity, is the real basis of all such arguments. If wrong occurs to the slave in consequence of emancipation, the slave-holder is not responsible for it, any more than he is responsible for the wrongs which arise to other people who have their rights. The plea of retaining the slave for his benefit, if good in this case, would justify us in seizing upon the liberties of any other class of men, when, in our judgment, their interests demand such seizure — thus subjecting every inalienable right to the caprice, the rapacity, the ignorance, and the wickedness of lawless intermeddling.

CHAPTER VIII.

SLAVERY NEVER THE RESULT OF NECESSITY.

As " drowning men catch at straws," we find slave-holders and their apologists much inclined to extenuate their conduct by the plea of necessity. When driven from the fallacy that slave-holding is an act of mercy, they try to sustain themselves by a sort of fatalism. It is not wonderful that slave-holders should resort to this method of justification, but it is strange that Christian Churches should be misled by the specious pretence. Men, strongly imbued with the spirit of reform, and deadly hostile to slavery, have often contented themselves with resolving that all voluntary slave-holders should be excluded from the Church. This is as much as to say that there may be a class of slave-holders who are involuntary, and, therefore, innocent. All such distinctions are exceedingly futile ; they have neither theoretical nor practical consistency. We might as well talk of involuntary cannibalism. But we will examine some of the alleged causes of the necessity in question.

1. It is said " the present generation of slave-holders were born under the system of slavery, and have no control over it — their condition was pre-determined, and they are not responsible for its evils." Now this is in part true, but does not at all exculpate the slave-holder. It is no more true of slavery than

of other sins, that men are born under their influence, and crippled by their antiquity and their prevalence. And if the plea of necessity is good in this case, it is good against all reform. Suppose Sabbath-breaking or lying had been sanctioned everywhere for centuries, would the present generation be at liberty to consider themselves hopelessly entangled? Could they not break away from these sins, notwithstanding the evil example of their ancestors, and all the effects of vicious habits and vicious associations? None will deny that they could and should, without the least hesitation. Why, then, shall we tolerate the sin of slavery as we tolerate no other sin? Or, is slavery not a sin?

We do not dispute that the hereditary character of slavery has made the work of emancipation more difficult. In many respects, the present race of slave-holders are eminently unfitted for the work of emancipation. They lack habits of industry, the love of liberty, the spirit of philanthropy, a knowledge of men and things, social advantages, and, above all, a government free from the disorders induced by oppression. But still, none of these things, nor all of them together, render the work impossible. Slave-holders are not worse off, in this respect, than other sinners. The drunkard is poorly prepared for reform— degraded, diseased, impoverished, and impelled by an insatiable appetite, he is anything but fitted for the arduous work of temperance. And yet we do not excuse him from the attempt, nor deem his efforts unlikely to succeed. That the slave-holder is predesti-

nated to continue in sin, cannot be true, for God has
commanded all men to repent, and we must either
deny that slave-holding is sin, or conclude that the
slave-holder should abandon the practice at once.

2. "The slaves, being property, could not be given
up without impoverishing their owners, and ruining
the country." This, we apprehend, is the most for-
midable objection. Emancipation is a question of
dollars and cents. All the necessity in the case is of
a pecuniary character. But just this difficulty occurs
in some form in reference to every sin. When Paul
preached at Ephesus against idolatry, none opposed
him more vehemently than Demetrius, who "made
silver shrines for Diana." His emphatic, "Sirs, ye
know that by this craft we have our wealth," revealed
the true secret of his zeal. Superstition was profitable to him. If vice itself is not always profitable,
there is always a class of people who make a liveli-
hood by pandering to vice, and these cannot reform,
because it cuts off their ill-gotten gains. The same
is true of slave-holders. Some would, no doubt, lose
all their property, and the whole country would, for a
time, nominally have less wealth, by ceasing to inven-
tory human beings as property, but is this any sufficient reason for slave-holding? Does increase of
wealth justify the crime of robbery? If so, the dis-
tiller should continue his business, even though myriads die, and myriads more are stripped of their all, to
fill his coffers. The robber should continue to rob,
and the thief should retain his stolen property, if
slavery is no crime; for these have to encounter ex-

actly the same kind of necessity that presses upon the
slave-holder.

It has often been said that we must devise some
expedient to relieve the immense losses which the abolition of slavery would occasion, before we press the
question upon the South. If such an obligation exists,
it will not apply to one class of culprits only ; we are
equally bound to provide for any pecuniary losses
which other wicked men may sustain by " ceasing to
do evil." The argument has not a particle of force,
and ought never to be named where there is the least
reverence for Christianity. It supposes that money
is more necessary than virtue, and that men are under no obligation to reform, if they are likely to lose
property by so doing. A more blasphemous sentiment never had existence.

3. " The slaves could not take care of themselves."
All know that this part of the alleged necessity for
continued slave-holding is so far from being true, that
the slaves not only take care of themselves, but of
their masters too. In all slave-holding countries,
slaves are compelled to till the soil, and do almost
everything in the shape of manual labor. But the
declaration, idle as it is, has long been contradicted
by facts. Hundreds and thousands of free negroes,
scattered through the different States of the Union,
do provide for themselves, and quite as comfortably
as their brethren are provided for, who still remain in
bondage. This objection is too manifestly puerile to
claim further notice.

4. " The laws will not admit of emancipation."

Here, again, the necessity involves a direct conflict
with religion.   In a matter of justice to man, are human laws to have precedence of the law of God?   If
the slave ought to be free, it is in vain to tell us that
the law will not let him be free.   What right have
we to hold him, contrary to justice and brotherly kindness — laws of God, and paramount to all other laws?
The wicked, who neither fear God nor regard man,
may put forth such objections, but no Christian can
do it with decency.   We are aware that the slave-
holding States have sought to perpetuate slavery, by
throwing embarrassments in the way of emancipation.
But, as yet, these obstacles are easily overcome, where
there is the slightest disposition to do right.   The
slaves are endowed with the power of locomotion;
they are not like trees, which cannot move, and must,
therefore, remain always in the same place.   Hence,
if their owners wish to set them free, they have only
to send them, or go with them, to a land of liberty —
happily, in many instances, not remote.   This we
mention the more readily, as the slaves themselves are
much inclined to show that emancipation is practicable, in spite of the laws and the owner also.   Masters,
though under some restrictions, still have the right to
go where they will with their property ; and, as slaves
are being constantly driven in gangs, all through the
various slave States, for the purpose of trade, they
certainly might be driven to the free States, if their
owners had any disposition to enfranchise them.   The
plea of legal embarrassments is wholly groundless in
itself, as against emancipation; for, though it may

NEVER THE RESULT OF NECESSITY.

retard, it cannot, possibly, prevent the master's power to manumit.

5. "The slaves refuse to leave their masters." It is barely possible that, in some instances, slaves are so ignorant and worthless, as not to know the value of liberty, or care to preserve it. Such cases occur in free countries, and it is not surprising if they are still more numerous among a people who, for many generations, have been denied all cultivation. How should they know what freedom is, and what its value to man? Have they ever been taught to value liberty, except by feeling the pains of oppression? No: but they have always been told that slavery was the best for them — that God made them to be slaves, and would send them to hell if they sought to be free. Is it strange, then, that with such teaching, and such advantages, some slaves should say they preferred not to be free? Would it not be contrary to all experience, if such an education produced — unless by reaction — a love of liberty? Be it then, that many of these poor, degraded creatures are ready, like Esau, to sell their birthright for a mess of pottage. This very foolishness of choice — this worse than bestial lowness of desire — is the master's crime! He has crushed the soul till its manhood has gone, and only the brute remains. We do not doubt that slavery is omnipotent for evil — it can kill out all the nobler instincts of the man, and probably has done so in many instances. We have no hesitation in conceding the triumphs of the institution in this line; but it is altogether impossible for us to conceive how any humane mind

could urge such a reason for the continuance of slavery.

It would be absurd, however, to suppose that this state of things is general among the slave population. In particular instances, the love of liberty may have expired, but the large and continually increasing number of fugitives from slavery, shows that the instinctive desire of freedom is still rampant in the hearts of the enslaved. The record of these escapes, if it could be written out, would prove that bondmen have, not unfrequently, a just appreciation of human rights, an intolerable loathing of bondage, a chivalrous courage, and indomitable perseverance. So strong is the tendency to liberty, that it requires the utmost vigilance of their oppressors to keep them from self-emancipation. If the slaves do not wish to be free, what mean the laws against education? And why are slave-holders so much in fear of insurrection? We need nothing more than the laws of the slave States, to establish the fact that the slaves are not contented, and do not remain willingly in slavery. This iniquitous legislation testifies for the slave, and contradicts the assertion of all who maintain that he has no wish to be free. Kept, he may be, but it can only be done by degrading him to a brute, and denying him, as far as possible, all opportunities to escape. The argument may be applied to slaves with little variation. They are slaves, but not from necessity. It may be hazardous for them to seek freedom — they may fail, or, perhaps, die in the attempt. But has not freedom always been purchased at this price?

Ask our Revolutionary patriots if peril did not surround them at every step. It was on sanguinary battle-fields, that they gained what the slave pants to enjoy. They endured all manner of sufferings — confiscation, poverty, reproach, war, and death, to secure a more perfect liberty. Yes, even the Father of his Country stood exposed to the traitor's doom, and had to console himself with the belief that "his neck was not made for a halter." There were men who would not have scorned to hang the immortal Washington, because he sought to augment his own and his country's freedom; and there are men who would kill the slave for emulating his noble example. The danger is undeniable, and so is the duty to meet it fearlessly. If slaves cower beneath the lash, and refuse to die for their rights, they seal their own doom. Such men refuse liberty on the only terms ever granted to man. They are not worthy of freedom, or they would be willing to pay its price. No necessity lies upon them, but such as has always been the attendant of noble aspirations.

Should any question the right of the slave to assert his freedom, and break away from his chains, we must remind them that the difficulty, whether theological or political, is not confined to the slave. The time was, when our ancestors were enthralled, and we have no doubt they did well in striking for liberty; and, even now, millions of the old world have our sympathies in their efforts to throw off hoary despotism. Why do we approve of our own freedom, and of the prospective emancipation of European sufferers, if these achievements have waged war upon the rights of others? We must, to be consistent, go back to servitude; for some master's property was injured when our fathers escaped from serfdom. But we scarcely need reply to an argument which denies the right of progress, and assumes that it is wrong to claim our own God-given rights. Slaves are as much entitled to rise in the scale of political, moral, and social improvement, as other human beings. It would require a special revelation to exempt them from the common immunities of our nature. They are weighed down by no fatality — cut off by no decree of God; they may be, and ought to be, what others are — free and independent. Long years have not sanctified the barbarous cruelty and base injustice which first enslaved them; they are as free, to-day, to assume the rights of men, as if there never had been a slave in the world. No necessity binds either master or slave to this guilty course. On the contrary, if both do not instantly reform, they contemn religion, and outrage all the maxims of political rectitude. They virtually say, that the gospel shall not raise the fallen, nor sanctify the depraved — that the reign of error and sin shall be perpetual, and the kingdom of God shall never come — that wrong is right, or that right is but the accident of power triumphing over innocence, manhood, liberty, and religion. Necessity, then, in this regard, is no other than perverseness of will.

PART II.

THE RELATION OF SLAVERY TO THE CHURCH.

THE relation of slavery to the Church is, undoubtedly, the same as that of all other great crimes — a relation of utter antagonism. At first view, it hardly seems necessary to dwell upon so palpable a truth; having shown the moral character of slavery, it looks like a work of supererogation, to formally discuss its ecclesiastical relations. But, bad as slavery is acknowledged to be, there are many who insist upon its continuance in the Church. They object to any rule expelling slave-holders, or preventing their admission to Church-fellowship. Under these circumstances, it becomes necessary to take up the subject in its religious bearings. Slavery, though conceded to be a sin, is not conceded to be such a sin as stamps the character inevitably with infamy. It is considered a venial fault, or, rather, no fault at all, in the Church-member, and the cry of fanaticism and persecution is raised whenever an attempt is made to drive it out of the Church, as we drive out other crimes. It is a sin in the State, but not in the Church; it is a sin of the State, and not of the Church; it is wrong in politics, and right in religion. Yes, right — for to such lengths is the matter carried. The advocates of slavery do not hesitate to declare that slave-holding is a virtue — a religious duty. This throws upon us the necessity of showing that slavery is fatal to Christian character, and to the existence of the Church.

———•———

CHAPTER I.

SLAVES CANNOT BE CHRISTIANS.

WE do not mean to say that slaves cannot be converted, and become Christians. They are, probably, as open to conversion as other people, and, when favored with the means of grace, no doubt many of them become true converts. But we mean to say, that Christianity strikes the slave law dead — that the slave is virtually emancipated by his conversion. Slaves may be converted, but they are not converted slaves; they may " abide as they are called," so far as the form or letter of the slave law is concerned, but they come under the power of a higher law, which exacts of them service incompatible with slavery. Neither do we assert that a slave cannot be saved as a heathen. If he acts up to the light of nature, and is denied all opportunity of becoming ac-

quainted with the gospel, he stands on the same ground
as the better class of heathen, concerning whom we
have hope. But the salvation of infants, idiots, and
heathen, is not the result of any Christianizing influence exerted upon them in this life.

Our reasons for believing that the slave cannot be
a Christian, are the following:

1. Slavery unmakes the man. The slave is a thing,
and not a man; he is not known as a man — he is
not permitted to act as a man. Having been declared
by the law to be a chattel, he is not allowed to be
anything more, nor is it possible for him to be anything more, while the law remains in force against
him, except by incurring martyrdom. This sad necessity of sinking below the organic elements of his
nature, utterly excludes Christianity. A thing — a
chattel — an article of traffic, has no responsibility.
Moral character is never affirmed of mere things;
manhood is an essential concomitant and condition of
religion. Conversion brings the slave up from his
degradation, and re-instates him among the human
species, in spite of the law. The Christian, therefore,
is not a slave, in the eye of the law, because he is not
a thing; his caste — his humanity — which the slave
code had taken from him, is restored by the law of
God. Now, if Christianity does thus bring back the
slave's manhood, it is in direct conflict with the law
which took it away; the lesser law yields to the greater, and the slave, by becoming a Christian, becomes
also a man. Did the slave law make provision for
humanity, then human beings might be slaves, and

still be Christians; but no provision being made for
the slave to be more than a thing, Christianity interferes to relieve him from the grasp of unrighteous
authority, and place him in a position of moral responsibility.

2. A slave can have no higher master. The law
gives the owner supreme control. The slave has not
a single reserved right. He is as destitute of all
rights whatsoever as a brute, or even any inanimate
object.

Now, the point in dispute is, whether one human
being can be thus subject to another human being,
and still be a Christian. We maintain that it is impossible. 1. Because "no man can serve two masters"—that is, two supreme masters. If the slave
must obey man, whatever he may command, he cannot obey God, unless upon the supposition that human
and divine commands are always in accordance with
each other, which is too improbable to be entertained
for a moment. 2. But apart from this, it is impossible that any Christain should be under supreme obligation to man. The idea of such obligation, is essentially anti-Christian. It cancels the claims of the
Creator, in a way at once atheistic and unceremoni-
ous. It destroys the possibility of religion, for the
very object of the gospel is to bring men — slaves and
slave-holders not excepted — to obey God as their
supreme Lord and Law-Giver. 3. Every Christian,
by the act of conversion, is made a subject of Christ's
kingdom. "One is your master, even Christ." This
subjection to Christ, brings the individual into new

relations, and necessarily destroys all obligation to obey man in anything which is contrary to the law of God. The slave is no longer " wholly subject to the will of another" human being. He is even free from the evil propensities of his own corrupt nature, which had previously enslaved him, no less than the civil law. Hence, it is truly said of the Christian that he is " free indeed."

When men are converted, slavery is broken down — the master can no longer control them, except in things lawful to be done. This, we need not say, is a serious abridgment of slavocratic despotism.

Bondmen, as well as freemen, must obey God in all things, and if the former, with this necessity resting upon them, can still be chattels, and obedient to man in everything, we have no objection. But it is altogether an abuse of language to call such a state slavery; it is slavery only in name. We might as well call him a Christian who merely bears the Christian name, but performs none of the duties which it implies.

3. The slave cannot cultivate his powers of body or mind as the law of God requires. Education is denied him, and if rest, or food, or clothing, sufficient to preserve health, is allowed, it is only because the want of these might depreciate his value as a working animal. The less mind the slave has the better, provided only he knows enough to work. But this, however well it may subserve the peace and stability of slave-holding communities, does not meet the wants of human nature. Development and culture

are requisite to that enlarged usefulness for which
the Christian is taught to aspire. He must not rest
contented with doing some good, but is obliged to use
all his talents or be condemned as an unfaithful stew-
ard. A blight is upon him that will sink him to the
pit, unless we suppose the wicked law under which
he is held can be plead as a justification of ignorance.
But the hope of such justification is utterly futile;
for, if applicable in this case, it is in every other; if
ignorance may be excused because the master prohibits knowledge, so may Sabbath-breaking, falsehood, and dishonesty.

4. The slave cannot have a conscience. His own
convictions of duty are wholly discarded. He may
think it right to worship God, to pray, and to be personally pure; but the master has absolute power over
him in all these particulars. Every abomination
which the master sees proper to tell his slave to commit,
the slave is bound to practice. The female must give
herself up to pollution, the mother must forsake her
children, and the wife her husband. And all, of every
age and sex, are bound to forsake their God, and do
any manner of wickedness that their masters may require. Here the conflict begins, and Christianity
strips the slave instantly of all the irresponsibility and
degradation which the slave law entails upon him —
it abrogates the slave law, and makes the slave a man,
and clothes him with all the responsibilities and immunities of a man. Accordingly, when St. Paul sent
Onesimus back to Philemon, he bid the latter receive
the former " not now as a servant, but above a ser-

vant, a brother beloved." Such is the effect of religion in every case; the convert is snatched from the clutches of human authority, though not always emancipated from human power. In like manner, death reigns for a time over the body after the soul is pardoned. The body of the once slave may still be within reach of the slave-holder, but the spirit is free, and the free spirit will keep the enslaved body from all sin, in spite of the world, the flesh and the devil.

5. Slaves cannot perform either conjugal, or parental, or filial duties. They cannot, because all power to discharge these duties is lodged with the master, and made dependent upon his will. He may, at any moment, imprison, sell, or separate those on whom such obligations rest, and thus cause them to violate the law of God. But slavery knows nothing of marriage or of the relations to which it gives rise — it does not admit the slave to these hallowed duties — it resolutely ignores his right to participate in them. Husband and wife, son and daughter, are terms applicable to human beings, but the slave is not a human being, and, therefore, has no interests of this kind. We ask, is it possible that a Christian should thus, at the bidding of man, waive these sacred claims? Can he be a Christian, and stand in this doubtful attitude to duties which God has laid upon him? we answer, unhesitatingly, No. These obligations having been imposed by the Creator, cannot be removed by human legislation.

6. Slaves cannot be Christians, because, in order to slavery, they must part with the humanity which God

has given them, and in doing so, they commit sin.
No man has any right to surrender, in this manner,
the endowments received from his Creator. We receive our powers as a sacred trust, and are held responsible for them. If they are relinquished at the
bidding of man, the divine law is treated with contempt. It is here that the slave incurs guilt. He
parts with a treasure, of which he was constituted, if
not the sole, yet the principal guardian, and for which
he must account to his Maker. No man can thus de-
base himself, and be innocent. Men are created that
they may be men; and if they sink down to mere
things, and become disqualified for the duties of humanity, they cannot escape the guilt of deserting their
post in life. We are well aware that the slave law is
imperative and clamorous; it clutches, and threatens
to swallow its victims alive and " whole, as those that
go down to the pit :" but all this is no sufficient apology. The slave may have to elect between death
and obedience to his God, or to the constitutional law
of his nature; but, in this necessity, he only stands
beset by the same difficulty which attends all other
men, whenever danger lies in the path of duty. "He
that departeth from iniquity maketh himself a prey."
Either the slave is under no obligation to use his faculties, or he sins by refraining from their use. We
believe the obligation rests upon him as fully as upon
other men, and that in consenting to be less than
man, he wickedly debases himself, and, therefore,
cannot be a Christian.

The argument, in form, stands thus: Christians

must obey the law of God; but slaves cannot obey the law of God; therefore, slaves cannot be Christians.

As we have advanced this sentiment editorially, it has met with considerable remonstrance, and some have denounced it in no measured terms. The following may be taken as a sample:

"The Northern Christian Advocate has made a new discovery in relation to the institution of slavery. It is now ascertained that the relation is equally fatal to master and servant, and that *submission* on the part of the slave, as certainly and effectually excludes him from a right to the fellowship of the Church, as the holding him in slavery does his master. This new theory, horrible as it is, will have a host of advocates, both in the ministry and membership of the Northern Church. Reason, experience, and even the authority of Revelation, can present no effectual barrier to such a fearful delusion. We may hope, at least, for a check to its progress in that principle of *reaction* which is the *safety-valve* of the universe."

The above is an extract from a recent letter of Bishop Soule to the editor of the Southern Christian Advocate. However horrible our position may be, it is impregnably just. No man has attempted to disprove it. Nor is the discovery a new one. It was known at least as long ago as the days of Homer.

> "Jove fixed it certain that whatever day
> Makes man a slave, takes half his worth away."
> (*Odyssey*, Book xvii.)

All we have ever affirmed is, that Christianity necessarily raises man above the condition of a brute. It exacts of him duties which a chattel cannot perform. It imparts to him an inspiration and an improvement which break through the trammels of civil authority, and make every slave converted a "brother beloved." It makes him the "Lord's free man," "an heir of God," and "joint heir with Christ." But the slave law says the slave is "as nothing, as dead, as a quadruped." It accordingly denies him the rights of a man, and seeks to obliterate from his nature all traces of manhood. Christianity, on the other hand, tries to develop the manhood in man—to bring out the noblest qualities of his soul, and build him up in wisdom and holiness. And in order to this, it must necessarily free him from all obligation to do wrong, whoever may command it.

Between slavery and Christianity there is, therefore, an eternal antagonism. Bishop Soule thinks it horrible, that a man cannot submit to be stripped of his manhood and of his obligation to God, and still be a Christian. And he will, perhaps, allege that the claims of heaven are graduated to man's temporal circumstances, so that of the slave nothing more is required than obedience to his master in all things. But we totally deny that this requisition of obedience to masters, involves an obligation to do the slightest wrong. The slave may not break the Sabbath, nor lie, nor steal, at the bidding of his master — hence it follows that a slave, by his conversion, is made free from the power of man, whereinsoever that power is contrary to the will of God. Even Bishop Soule will admit that the master's power is limited in this respect. This limitation, however, is fatal to the whole system of slavery. For, if the master may require nothing wrong, then the slave is free to do his whole duty — free to be a man and a Christian, in spite of the law which makes him a chattel. This is practical abolition. The law may remain, but it is a dead letter. The slave is emancipated by the gospel of Christ.

We maintain that the obligations of slavery and the obligations of Christianity are diametrically opposite — that slavery has excluded humanity, and with it, the possibility of religion — that conversion, by restoring the functions of humanity, virtually annihilates the slave law. And so far as we have any knowledge of slave character, this view is sustained by actual occurrences. Slaves have held fast their integrity by resisting the unrighteous requirements of their masters, and suffering the consequences. Unless the slave States are greatly belied, many of the sable sons and daughters of Africa have preserved their virtue only by preferring martyrdom to apostacy. That is to say, they have thrown off slavery — have "resisted unto blood, striving against sin." Uncle Tom, the fictitious hero of Mrs. Stowe's celebrated work, is only a familiar illustration of the common fate of invincible piety, under the workings of the horrible slave system. In every such case, religion or slavery must give way ; if the master cannot corrupt the slave into obedience, the slave bows to death, and asserts his freedom by gaining a martyr's crown.

Should it be said the slave may have a good master — one who will both treat him kindly and require nothing wrong of him, and that, in such a case, the evils we have mentioned would not exist : we reply that the supposition yields the whole question ; it concedes that the slave law may be inoperative — the very thing for which we contend. In so far as the slave-master treats his slave as a human being, he treats him contrary to the slave law, and thus practically nullifies the law. All rights accorded to the slave are violations of the law by which he is held in bondage ; if he is not treated as a brute, he is not treated according to the character which the statute gives him, nor according to the power vested in the master. That anomalous instances occur in which the authority of the master is not exercised, we are ready to admit ; but this only confirms the truth of our position — it shows that the law must be suspended to make way for Christianity. We do not, by any means, deny that the master may cease from his unrighteous exactions and give his slaves a chance to become Christians ; we only insist that he must so cease, or that the slaves must discard his authority, if they are ever converted.

What, then, becomes of slavery ? Is not the chattel at once a man ? and is there not laid on him the duties of a man ? Has he not a God ? and are not all his powers of body and mind to be supremely devoted to his God ? Is he not under just the same obligations in this respect as other men ? and if so, can he, more than any other man, submit to anything which contravenes the will of Heaven ? Now, unless these questions can be answered in the negative, the controversy is settled — slavery expires as Christianity progresses, and the presence of the latter displaces the former, as surely as light displaces darkness.

We have dwelt the longer on this point, because it has too commonly been supposed that future happiness might recompense the slave for present misery. Slavery has been considered no barrier to religion, and the slave not much to be commiserated, since another and better life would make ample amends for his wretchedness in this. But the case is widely varied, if slavery cuts off eternal as well as temporal prospects. It is our deliberate conviction that the slave is ruined for both worlds.

"Sin kills beyond the tomb."

And the sin of slavery kills quite as certainly as any other sin. If the slave could die into freedom and felicity, we would not dispute about the injuries inflicted upon him here ; but when it is understood that his condition is no less hopeless for Heaven than for earth, his fate appeals to Christian sympathy with no common force. Heaven is not to be peopled with chattels. The slave-holder cannot console himself with the reflection that the evils which he occasions will end with this life. His brutes here will be brutes hereafter. Having driven the poor slave from all vantage ground, and denied him all opportunities of improvement, till the grave closed over him — having, in short, defeated every purpose for which probationary life was given, he must not expect the victims of his cruelty to be recompensed by the joys of Heaven. For Heaven, preparation is necessary, but this preparation the slave may not acquire. It would no doubt be very convenient if a portion of mankind could be degraded to utter brutality through all their lives, and then pass safely into Paradise ; oppression and spoliation might be pushed to any length without endangering the soul, and Heaven would become the receptacle of all the cast-off and worn-out *things* which inexorable death had placed beyond the oppressor's reach. The slave-holder might then bargain and sell, and drive his property while life lasted, and God would kindly take it at the grave, and enthrone it in everlasting light. But such is not the economy of Providence. The gospel of Christ provides that the redeemed shall be saved here ; it provides that the men admitted to Heaven shall be men on earth — men purified and trained for that holy place.

It is this soul murder—this double and eternal death, which renders the institution of slavery so horrible. The blow is professedly aimed only at the body ; but in order to make the physical powers of the human being available for this awful service, it is necessary to enfeeble and extinguish, as far as may be, the intellectual and moral faculties. This is done by positive edicts against education, and against all the more efficient means of improvement: it is further done by the most abject and suffocating restrictions of personal liberty, and by inhibiting every right, relation, and pursuit calculated to impart mental force. And as if determined that nothing should be wanting to complete his ruin, the slave is deliberately cast from the pale of humanity. What the chances of such a

being are for religious culture, is but too evident.
With this deadening process going on against his nobler nature — with the law interdicting his right to be
human, he certainly cannot be expected to rise in the
scale of excellence. If he does rise, it must be in
defiance of the circumstances by which he is sur-
rounded. In obedience to the higher instincts of his
nature—not quite obliterated by the extinguishing
appliances of slavery — he must assert his humanity
and become a man.

Finally, however hard it may seem to un-christian-
ize the slave for remaining a slave after his conversion, there is no other alternative. We must either
deny that human beings are under obligation to cultivate their powers, and discharge the duties incident
to the several relations of life, or hold slaves, as we
hold all other men, bound to act up to their human
nature, and not as mere brutes, the only character
which the law assigns them. Slaves should be men,
or they should not; if the former, they must of necessity throw off the trammels of the slave code,
though at the peril of life; but if the latter is true,
then their obligations are canceled, and the virtues
required of men are a dead letter to all in bonds.
Dare any take this position? Dare any say that souls
may be trained for Heaven, without being taught to
obey the law of God in all things? We admit that
slaves may be converted, but their conversion is one
thing, and their Christian culture another. We have
no right to infer that they may live and enjoy religion
out of the pale of humanity, because such a state

does not debar them from repentance. The greatest sinners may be converted—the drunkard, the liar, the swearer, and the adulterer—but can they live in the practice of the same things after their conversion? Certainly not. No more can the slave be "a servant of man" in anything contrary to holiness. His own moral integrity thenceforth becomes to him of sovereign consequence — he is the Lord's free man, and none may oblige him to sin. We must not be deceived by appearances. No mere professions—no religious feelings or exercises, are to have weight as proofs of religion, where the life is not right. If the slave still remains a submissive tool of his owner — if his obligation to God is not considered paramount to everything else, he is not a Christian. But if his allegiance to God is sacred, he is not a slave. Men may call him a slave, but the mastery over him is in Heaven.

CHAPTER II.

SLAVE-HOLDERS CANNOT BE CHRISTIANS.

IF slavery incapacitates the slave for religion, it equally incapacitates the slave-holder. The disastrous effects of the system are, indeed, even more conspicuous in the latter case than in the former. That the robber suffers a greater moral injury than the robbed, admits of no dispute. But this principle applies to all who commit crime, and to the slave-holder as truly as to other criminals. It is not denied that the slave-holder may be converted and become a Christian; he is not beyond the reach of grace, but in order to obtain it, he must renounce his sins. The drunkard may become a Christian, yet not without putting away his drunkenness; mercy is gained only by repentance. Still further, it is not denied that men may be Christians and be merely technical slave-holders — that is, slave-holders according to the letter, but not according to the spirit of the law. As a mere formalist is not a Christian, so one who only formally holds slaves is not a real slave-holder. In order to slavery, the law must be carried out; men must be regarded and treated as chattels, to the utter sacrifice of their personal freedom, and all the collateral rights of humanity. Having premised these things, we shall now present the argument against the religious character of slave-holders.

1. Slave-holders cannot be Christians, because slavery is sin. We are aware that this proposition appears to assume the point in dispute. But the objection is of no force, unless it can be shown that slavery is not a sin. We maintain that slavery is a sin, a great sin, and a sin under all circumstances: and if this position is impregnable — it ought to be made to bear up the question under consideration. That sin destroys Christian character, is indeed a plain truth; but there is a strange reluctance to apply it here. The law is acknowledged to be wicked, and slavery itself is pro-

nounced an abomination; but yet no blame is attached to the slave-holder — he is allowed to pass as the victim of circumstances — his sin is no sin, for the simple reason that the State is also involved in the crime. Did men look at the sin of slavery as they do at other sins, and hold all parties to a strict accountability for their participation in it, there would be little need of announcing a truth so palpable as that now before the reader. The argument itself is indisputable. The sinner cannot be a Christian. This is conceded by Dr. Fuller.

"That sin must at once be abandoned, is a proposition which admits of no debate. If slavery, then, be a sin, it should at once be abolished." (*Letters to Dr.* WAYLAND, *Letter* 1.)

Thus, it is only by denying slavery to be a sin, that its advocates pretend to claim a religious character for the slave-holder. And the denial extends not merely to slavery under certain circumstances, but to slavery *per se:* the institution must be pronounced right, if rightly used. But we have shown that it cannot be rightly used — that it is a crime in itself, and no more admits of improvement than murder or adultery.

The fact that a sinner cannot be a Christian, is all we insist upon, in this connection, as this fact fully sustains the conclusion to which we arrive — namely, that the slave-holder is not a Christian. The argument is valid, if the premises are good. Hence, no one will accuse us of unfairness, unless they, at the same time, reject the proofs which we have adduced to show the essential wickedness of slavery. Let those who stumble at the idea of unchristianizing slave-holders, remember that the conclusion is inevitable, if the premises which we have assumed are correct. That slave-holders cannot be Christians, is no arbitrary and harsh judgment, provided simply that slavery is a sin.

Why, then, shall the proposition at the head of this chapter be considered bold ? Why shall it be deemed uncharitable ? It amounts to no more than this — that sin is incompatible with religion. Slave-holders and their apologists admit this, and still profess to be shocked when we say that slave-holders are not Christians. They do not perceive, that in order to avoid this conclusion, they must absolutely deny the sinfulness of slavery, and that the argument is nothing more than the legitimate application of a truth, always insisted upon by the opponents of slavery — viz: that slavery is a sin. The Christian is required to be holy, and if slavery is unholy, it is plain to demonstration that no Christian can be a slave-holder. Let those who dispute our position, set themselves to demolish the foundation on which it rests. Let them show, if they can, the immaculateness of slavery — that it is neither sin, nor of sinful tendency. When they have done this successfully, we will acknowledge our argument unsound.

2. Slave-holders cannot be Christians, because slavery usurps the Divine prerogatives. No Christian can exercise unlimited control over another human being. The Christian is aware that himself, and all other men, are bound to obey the law of God, and he

cannot presume to exercise a power which he knows belongs to God alone. That the master has absolute, unlimited authority over the slave, is beyond question. The slave has no power to do anything contrary to the will of the master. Let it be ever so great a crime, in the sight of God or man, that is exacted of him, the right of resistance is equally denied. He is made to know that the master's will is his supreme law for both worlds. What the master commands — be it right or wrong — that he must do. Here, then, is the most absolute and unqualified tyranny of which it is possible to conceive. It sets at naught the divine supremacy, and renders man accountable, not to his God, but to a human owner — a slave-master. Such an assumption of authority is wholly unknown in any other relation of life. An attempt has been made to find something analogous in the authority of a husband over his wife, of a parent over his children, and of a monarch over his subjects; but the attempt is a failure. It is ridiculous to make such a comparison. The mild and limited authority belonging to these relations, has no resemblance to the brutal despotism of slavery. In the one case, there are always reserved rights, which operate as a check to abuses; in the other, there are no reserved rights whatever. The conscience of the wife, and the child, and the subject, is never surrendered to human authority; those who govern them, govern in subjection to a higher law, and it is always understood that a command to do wrong, emanating from such a source, would carry with it no obligation, inasmuch as God has forbidden

all wrong-doing. But the slave-holder's authority
has no qualification; his victim not being human, in
the eye of the law, is supposed to have no conscience
to preserve inviolate, and no soul to be endangered
by compliance with sinful requirements. The master
is, therefore, entrusted with supreme control, and the
slave bows to his every mandate, as to the decision of
his final Judge. There is a further difference, too
important to be overlooked : in the relations afore-
said, the persons occupy their true positions in the
social world—the wife was destined to be a wife, the
child to be a child, and the subject a subject; each is in
his appropriate place, and subject to such authority
only as is demanded by his natural position in
society. But not so with the slave; his powers must
be crushed to keep him degraded; the authority necessary in this case, must be so perfect that it will cut
off all return to manhood, and leave the man a brute
forever. It is no common power that the slave-holder
exercises; on him is devolved the dreadful work of
blasting the humanity of the negro, through every
scene in life, and in every possible relation to society.
He must execute the horrible purpose of the State ;
the State has placed the slave among brutes, and it is
the owner's business to keep him there. He is bound,
as a law-abiding citizen, to see that the design of the
government is not frustrated; he is entrusted with
the fearful responsibility of keeping the slave precisely what the law has made him—a thing, a chattel.

That no Christian can do this, without a forfeiture
of religious character, is just as obvious as it is that

no Christian can commit a variety of the highest crimes, one of which shall be the denial of a God. One of the first attributes of Christianity is, the acknowledgment of God in his several relations of Creator, Preserver, and Governor. Where this recognition of Divinity is wanting, there can be no religion. But slavery sets aside the authority of God, as completely as if he had never issued any command to the African. The slave is forbidden to be a man, and may neither know nor serve his God in the only relation which he was created to sustain. He may, it is true, if the master chooses, learn something of religion, but he must learn it out of character — learn it, not as a man and a member of society, but as one disinherited and forbidden to return to the common brotherhood of the human family. But even this, be it remembered, is completely optional with the master, and herein lies the grievous wrong. It was never designed that one human being should stand in such a relation to another human being as to nullify the Creator's supremacy. Yet slavery makes this relation necessary — it compels the owner to stand in the place of God, and exercise a power which does not belong to man. Even if the slave consented to the surrender of his powers in this manner, it would be wicked for the master to accept the surrender. How much more wicked, then, must it be when the wrong is inflicted by force! If the slave has no right to consent to be a slave, surely the master has no right to compel him to be one.

Before God, the slave and his owner stand on exactly the same ground, and one has just as much right as the other to interfere with any question of duty. Both are alike responsible to the Supreme authority for every act, and both must refrain from all improper coercion, or sink their Christian character. The slave-owner, however, cannot refrain, and still be the owner of human chattels ; if he refrains, his chattels immediately become men, and the slave law is a dead letter. If he fails to govern in everything — if he allows the slave to act as a man, and to choose what he will or will not do, then again the same result follows — the slave is virtually free, and the law is null. Thus a constant and unscrupulous usurpation of the slave's rights as a man, must be kept up, or slavery ceases of its own accord. But the Christian cannot usurp the rights of any — he must " render to all their dues ;" consequently he cannot be a slave-holder.

3. Slave-holders cannot be Christians, because slavery is a violation of the law of love. A Christian must love the colored man as himself, and must do to him as he would wish, circumstances being reversed, should be done to himself. Now, as " no man ever hated his own flesh," it is not possible for any one to wish for slavery — slavery for himself and children, through interminable generations. For this reason, every converted man will be utterly incapacitated to hold a slave. We do not say that he may not nominally and technically hold a slave, but we say he cannot really hold one. IIe will regard the relation as wicked, and will treat the law as a dead letter.

Let it be observed, then, that we place the non-slave-holding of Christians on the ground of actual incapacity. God has so constituted them that they cannot commit the abomination, and still retain the elements of their religious nature. In order to justification, they must not only renounce all desire to invade the rights of others, but actually attain to such a knowledge of right and wrong as will enable them to abstain from all unrighteousness. A Christian cannot be a pirate, because piracy is of the devil; and yet piracy is no worse than slavery. The laws of our country have long regarded the foreign slave trade as piracy; but the foreign slave-trade is no worse than the domestic, and the trade in slaves, whether foreign or domestic, is no worse than the simple ownership of slaves. Moral purity justly abhors the whole traffic, counting every part of it equally guilty — the seller, and the buyer, and the owner are all on the same ignominious level. Each and all consent to have and hold what honesty forbids — what is not their own, and cannot be, for the simple reason that eternal justice assigns it to the slave. The law of love will not allow the Christian to participate in this robbery; he may not even sanction it by his silence, much less by sharing, though it be ever so remotely, in the vile transaction. Rebuke, not participation, is demanded; but not rebuke alone. It is not enough that the Christian reproves such deeds of darkness by words; his acts, conservative of the slave's rights, must declare his heart-felt abhorrence of the abuse practiced upon his fellow man — though that

man be a slave. In a word, the Christian is so constituted that he must, of necessity, regard the slave as
a brother man, and treat him as such. He cannot
take advantage of a wicked law to oppress him, any
more than he can to murder him — he cannot perform
any one of all the several acts which are enjoined by
the slave code. To carry out such laws, demands another kind of being — one who feels himself under no
obligation to treat man as man — as a brother, for
whose welfare even the sacrifice of life, if it were
necessary, would be both a pleasure and a duty.

4. Christians cannot be slave-holders, because slavery depresses men. The Christian is bound to elevate
all around him, as fast as possible. No truth — no
principle in religion, is plainer than this : that all
men are to be cultivated and improved, as far as we
have power to do it. It becomes impossible, therefore, for a religious man to aid, either less or more, in
the work of degradation — he views the African as
his brother, and is compelled, by every consideration
of duty, to educate and improve him to the utmost
of his power. Hence he must accord to him all the
rights which the God of nature gave, and all the tender regards which the gospel of Christ enjoins. It
would be singular, indeed, if Christianity, after imposing the duty of culturing humanity — the humanity of all men — to the highest extent, had, nevertheless, excepted large classes, towards whom nothing
was due, but the most rigorous and systematic depression. Such an anomaly in religion there is not. No
portion of the human family is given up to ruin —

none are predestinated to the crushing influence of
slavery. Laws against education and liberty, against
marriage and the rights of property, against conscience and manhood, are laws against God ; they are
a direct attack upon Christianity, and must inevitably
be spurned by every believer in divine revelation.
Before a Christian can be a slave-holder, the law of
God must be repealed, in every particular affecting
the relations of man to man. The fraternal spirit,
now so conspicuous in all parts of the law, must be
utterly obliterated. When this is done, the work of
desolation can go on, but not before. Until then, the
obligations of the Gospel will make it impossible for
any Christian to join in a conspiracy with civil government against the rights of any man.

But may not the Christian become the depositary
of the slave's rights, and thus guard for the slave's
good, what the law had taken from him? Not at all.
As to any guardianship of such rights, it is absurd —
nay, more, impossible. No man can, innocently, be
the depositary of what belongs to another's manhood.
The slave must regain his rights before he can be a
man. None can act for him in this matter. God has
laid certain duties on the slave, as a man, and will
hold him — not his master — responsible for their
performance. The master cannot answer for any but
himself, in the day of judgment. Aside from the impossibility of this transfer of obligations, is the intrinsic guilt of the original transaction. The Christian slave-owner, by consenting to hold the slave as
a slave, endorses the conduct of the Legislature or

law-making power, and thus becomes as guilty as those who perpetrated the enactment. Can an honest man consent to be the depositary of stolen goods? He might, perhaps, for the purpose of restoring them to the owner, but not for a moment for any other purpose. The goods are not his, and never can be his; to retain them, therefore, an instant, except for the sole purpose of returning them to their owner, is to be partaker with the thief. We may render the case still plainer, by supposing the right in question to be, not that of personal freedom, but the right to life. Had the law, without cause, doomed the slave to death, could a Christian participate in the infliction? Could he become the depositary and administrator of this cruel power? All will see at once, that to do so would be murder. The government should be left to execute its own wicked laws, if they must be executed, for no honest man can lend himself to such a work.

The plea that Christians hold slaves to shield them from a worse fate, is altogether fallacious. No worse fate is possible. He that is a slave, has lost all he had to lose, except life, and that is his only in a very qualified sense. As an animal, he might suffer more in the hands of one master than in the hands of another. But his rights as a man are sacrificed to the same extent, whatever may be the character of his owner. The slave-owner who recedes from the property principle, does not execute the law, and in so far, is not a slave-owner. If the Christian respects his slave, and counts him a brother — as we contend he must do — the slave law is no longer in force, and he cannot be said to hold a slave. But if he does apply the law, and reduce the man to a chattel, what better is he than another — than the common run of slave-holders? It is no matter what hand does the deed, if it must be done. Robbery, committed by a pious man, is just as much robbery as if committed by a professional highwayman. The assassin's knife, plunged to the heart by the hand of a friend, is not less fatal than if driven there by the hand of an enemy.

The whole argument resolves itself into this proposition: Man was never made to be a slave, and whoever enslaves him, sins against God. There is no avoiding this conclusion, unless by assuming that a portion of mankind were created to be slaves, and nothing else. It must be right to degrade men, and keep them degraded forever, or slavery is a sin, and being a sin, it is forbidden, both to the Christian and all others. "He that committeth sin is of the devil."

5. The Christian cannot be a slave-holder, for the reason that slavery deranges and even annihilates those relations of man to man, and of men to God, which Christianity is especially designed to purify and conserve. One great object of the gospel is to restore fraternal feeling to mankind — to revive the principle of brotherhood, and blend nations and races together as one family. But we have seen that the slave-holder cannot conform to this design without sacrificing slavery — to treat the slave as "a brother beloved" is to raise him up to the rank of a man, and accord to him all the rights which belong to humani-

ty. But this is not all. The slave is intended for
marriage and its various responsibilities, as really as
other men. The conjugal and parental relations are
devolved upon him by the appointment of the Creator, and no man can lawfully crush him down so as to
render him incompetent to these positions. Again,
the slave is designed for citizenship, and must be permitted to act as a virtuous member of society. His
obligations in this respect are the same as those of
other citizens, and they are not to be canceled at the
bidding of any human authority. Yet further, his
relations to God and to eternity — or in other words,
his relations as a moral being — are precisely identical
with those of the rest of the human race. Slavery
makes the man a blank, so far as religious obligation
is concerned. He may pray, or do any other religious
duty, it is true, if the master permits; but the crime
consists in taking from him the right to do these things
of his own accord and without consultation. As a
man he is required to serve God, irrespective of human permission. He has an equal right with other
men in all these particulars; he has rights which no
Christian can either deny or grant. It would be
mockery to grant men the right to take care of their
children, or to pray, since God has formally commanded them to do these things, and no man has any right
to prevent their doing them. We might as well command the sun to rise or the winds to blow. Permission here is out of place — we have nothing to permit.
Where duty has been assigned by the Creator, either
by his written word, or by a law of our nature, it is a

wicked farce to superadd our leave for its performance, especially when, by so doing, we imply that the
right would not just as fully exist without such leave.
Every act of indulgence accorded by the real slave-
holder is a blasphemy. He re-enacts the law of God,
not reverently, and as a matter of solemn obligation,
but capriciously, and as Something that would have
no force but for his ratification. A higher insult to
divine authority cannot be conceived.

But aside from this mockery of granting men permission to obey God, slavery, by whomsoever administered, directly reverses all the established rules of
virtue and religion — it beats down the lowly, because they are low, the poor, because they are poor,
and the weak, because they are weak. This system,
instead of teaching men to "bear one another's burden's
and so fulfill the law of Christ," cruelly heaps upon
the helpless colored man all the disabilities that law
can impose, and dooms him to drag out life in the
character of a brute. Instead of raising him up, and
enduing him with advantages, as both religion and
humanity dictate, it strips him of even the natural
rights that God had conferred upon him in common
with mankind. Such a system must forever be intolerable to all upright minds. Christians can have no
more to do with it than they have to do with highway
robbery and murder. It is impossible to frame any
plea that shall excuse the slightest connection with
the abomination.

Here we leave the argument. If any can show its
unsoundness, let them do it. But until then, we shall

continue to regard slave-holders as necessarily excluded from the pale of Christianity. That they are not Christians, and cannot be, while continuing the practice of slavery, is to us just as plain as that the gospel of Christ is a system of benevolence. Did Christianity sanction rapine, violence, spoliation and oppression — did it set apart the African, or any other class of men, to receive as their only portion the utmost indignities that lawless power can inflict — did it command the believer to be the instrument of this infliction — and did it not enjoin us to love our neighbor as ourselves — then we might admit that slave-holding and religion could be united in the same person.

Perhaps some may think we have advanced far enough in this direction. But we must go one step further, however bold it may appear, and affirm that slavery and slave-holding are not only incompatible with religion, but with manhood itself. To be a slave, is to sink below the order of humanity into that of brutes. So that, religion aside, slavery is impossible to our nature — a man cannot be a man, " in any proper sense of the word," and be a slave.

The same is true of the slave-holder. He descends not only below religion, but below all the more honorable principles of humanity. For instance, it is dishonorable, even among men who make no pretensions to religion, to injure the weak and the defenceless, or to take advantage of women and children, the sick and the lame. But here is a poor, weak, ignorant African race, whose misfortunes appeal for sympathy to every honorable feeling of nature, and

for whose protection, common honor, to say nothing
of piety, demands that we should peril our lives, if
need be, and yet the slave-holder — we mean the bona fide slave-holder, makes these his prey! These
he attacks with all the ferocity of a beast, and strips
them of every right, merely because he can. Such
a being outrages the feelings which are congenial
to humanity, apart from the lofty maxims of Christianity.

So far, therefore, is it from being an act of te-
merity, or uncharitableness, to affirm that slave-holders cannot be Christians, that all consideration of their
pretensions to religion, is somewhat misplaced. It is
a condescension even to bestow the slightest attention upon claims so evidently preposterous. The
moral character of the slave-holder does not rise high
enough to entitle it to such investigation. A being
so fallen and depraved that all the nobler instincts
of his nature have ceased to operate, cannot be ranked
among Christians till he has been created anew, nor
among civilized men till he is greatly reformed. Such
brutality as makes women and children slaves for
life, is repugnant not only to religion and the civil
law, but to every manly sentiment, and necessarily
fixes an ineffaceable stain upon its foul perpetrator.
When such an one — forgetful how much more polluted he is than the common run of men — seeks to
be considered a Christian, then Satan himself may
aspire to the honors of saintship. Slavery is, in fact,
so gross an offence to humanity, that its removal is
the province of civilization rather than of religion.

CHAPTER III.

SLAVERY CANNOT EXIST IN THE CHURCH.

OF course, if neither slaves nor slave-holders can be Christians, slavery can have no existence in the Church of Christ. But we allude only to the true or invisible Church ; for sinners as well as saints may be members of the visible Church. Through the infirmity of human judgment, and the concealment of sin by those who practice it, the bad are often associated with the good in Church fellowship. But we are not, on this account, to suppose that all are alike Christians. Judas, though ranked with the apostles, was still only "a devil." The same is true of all the wicked, whatever may be their relation to the external Church. Our reasons for affirming that slavery cannot exist in the Church, are these :

1. The Church, to use the language of the Thirty-Nine Articles, is " a congregation of faithful men, in which the true word of God is preached," &c. Now, as has been shown in the previous chapter, no slave-holder can be a faithful man. He must be recreant to his duty as the friend of the oppressed, and the enemy of oppression — he must degrade those whom God would raise up — he must lend himself to the State, as an instrument of cruelty to accomplish designs which the gospel abhors. His own imagined justification may be that by thus doing, he mitigates, in some degree, the extreme evils which the slave

would otherwise suffer. But we have already shown the fallacy of this reasoning. The State has no right to oppress — no right to make slaves, and, therefore, cannot confer this right upon others. Let the case be varied ever so slightly, and all will see the monstrous absurdity of the thing. Suppose the State should enact that every man might swear profanely, or steal, or commit adultery, at his own option, and without any penalty or censure whatever; would the Christian thereby acquire any right to practice these vices? Could he participate in them because the civil law allowed him to do so? Most certainly he could not. But suppose, further, that the State enacted that these vices might be committed with additional circumstances of atrocity — such as swearing with unusual frequency, or with a needless multiplication of unlawful words, stealing what the thief does not want, or must destroy at once, committing adultery with females peculiarly happy in their domestic circumstances, or where the disgrace would fall with the greatest weight on the family connections. It would be natural for a conscientious man, if he should commit these sins at all, to do so without the aggravations here specified; but could he practice them even, if he strove to avoid the excess which the law enjoined? Above all, would he be justified in practicing them in this temperate manner, merely to prevent the excess of which others less conscientious, by taking advantage of the law, might commit? For him to do so, would be " to do evil that good might come" — a doctrine pointedly reprobated by the word of God.

But we will suppose further, that all contingency is out of the question—these vices must be committed; either through the corruption of human nature, or from some other cause, such "offences must come." Does this necessity afford any pretext for their commission? By no means. The "woe" is upon "him by whom the offence cometh." The Christian himself is under no necessity of this kind, and he may not volunteer to do wickedness because others will certainly do greater wickedness until God converts them. The slave-holder, therefore, whatever may be his intentions, is doing an unlawful work, and consequently is not in the Church. He is a worker of iniquity, and the Lord knows him not. He may be outwardly a church-member; he may have prophesied, cast out devils, and done many wonderful works in the Lord's name, but still is not a Christian, because he does not the will of God in abstaining from all unrighteousness.

2. Slavery cannot exist in the Church, because the Church is holy. We talk of excluding slavery from the Church, as though it had really gained a footing there. But we might just as well talk of excluding drunkenness and murder from the Church — sins which all know preclude Christian character, and with it exclusion from the spiritual Church. He that commits these things may, indeed, have a name to live, but is dead while he liveth — spiritually and religiously dead, having at most only a dead form of godliness. Slavery never had a place in the true Church, and never can have, till crime ceases to

be an impediment to admission into the fold of Christ.
So long as "putting off the old man with his deeds"
is a condition of church-membership, so long must
slave-holders, with other sinners, "remain in the congregation of the dead." The slave-holder may felici-
tate himself on his admission to the visible Church,
but this shall avail him nothing — his name must be
written in the Book of Life, before he can be considered in the Church, or have any ground of hope.
Hence the Church is placed far above corruptions of
this character; it cannot be invaded by a lax-admin-
istration of human authority. Men may decree that
slavery is no bar to religion, but this makes the way
to heaven no wider — it will not introduce the oppressor into the family of Christ.

3. But, strictly speaking, slavery is impossible in
the Church anywhere — yes, impossible even in the
visible Church. In order to have slavery, we must
have a state of things altogether inimical to the
nature of religion. Popery, by taking on a political element, and by assuming unlawful power, has
become more nearly a civil than a religious institution. It is a political league, not a Church. The
same is true of any evangelical Church, when it in-
corporates slave-holding. There must be a lower
caste — a class of persons distinguished from others by
the denial of privileges intended for all. The slave
in the Church is still doomed to ignorance, dependence, servility, concubinage, and sale — he is the
same chattel as before, and follows the laws of property just as necessarily as he ever did. The owner-

ship of men by members of the Church, is an innovation fatal to that equality and fraternal regard peculiar to such organizations. A Church thus corrupted, deserves to be considered as a political oligarchy — it is a Church only in name.

4. It cannot be in the Church, because a genuine church-membership is in theory and spirit subversive of all unrighteousness. Every wicked act must be disclaimed — abhorred. All usurpation and improper control over others, is rendered impossible by the very constitution of the Christian. He might, as a man of the world, buy and sell men, or as a merely formal professor, he might "lord it over God's heritage," but not as a true Church member. Were there no rule against the practice, he could not conform to it, inasmuch as he has no heart to such a work. The Christian's kindly disposition is not the only preventive of slavery; he is, by his position in the Church, far too much penetrated with a sense of his own infirmity, unworthiness and dependence, to attempt the exercise of slavocratic functions. A community living under the immediate eye of God, with their affections set on things above, must be illy prepared for the slightest participation in that greedy absorption of power which marks slave-holding. Having been pardoned and restored to the divine favor wholly by grace, how can such people prove so ungracious as to rob their fellow men of a single particle of their natural rights? In the church, each has a master, and each for himself "to his own master standeth or falleth." No improper or unholy interference is pos-

sible here, without such a derangement as assimilates
the Church to other corrupt institutions.   Should it
be said that this argument proves too much, from the
fact that there are wicked men in *all* Churches, the
answer is, then all Churches are in so far corrupt.   A
true Church is not made up partly of the good and
partly of the bad, for none but the good — the children of God — are rightfully members of even the
visible Church.   Why do we exclude sinners, if they
have a right in the Church ?   If they have no right
there, the Church is injured by their presence, and
ought to consult her own safety by separating " the
precious from the vile."

5. If slavery may be in the Church militant, then
it may be in the Church triumphant. Nothing should
be tolerated on earth that is not holy enough for
Heaven.   But can we conceive of slavery in Paradise ? Will the disgusting, barbaric system transmit
itself into the immediate presence of God, and there
riot in eternal oppression ? If men may be fit for
Heaven, and yet be slaves or slave-holders, — if, with
this character, they may occupy a place in the Church
here, we cannot see why they may not hold these relations through eternity.   They certainly will have
the same character in a future state that they had in
this — if they die slaves and slave-holders, we know
not what shall make them more pure, or place them
in different relations in the world to come.   These
relations being good enough for time, may be pronounced good enough for the eternal state.   Such is
the astonishing absurdity which must follow from ad-

mitting that slavery may have existence in the Church.

6. The constitution of the Church, however, is decisive upon the point — it determines the relations of members, in spite of all disturbing causes. Men cannot come into the house of God as they please, and make it what they please; the power to effect a revolution is not in their hands. Here, at least, in his own house, "the Lord sitteth King forever." The members of the Church are brethren; they have one master, even Christ, and all are brethren of one family. This excludes the possibility of slave ownership. All are Christ's, and none can claim aught as his own that belongs to another. There are no lawless, no unjust, no unbrotherly acquisitions or possessions here. The law of brotherhood is the great organic law of the Church; men can enter into its communion as brothers, but in no other capacity. They can neither buy, nor sell, nor own one another, nor yet those out of the Church, any more than children of the same family can buy, or sell, or own each other as chattels personal.

7. To the Church, slavery is and must be unknown, except as one of the most criminal and grievous outbreakings of human depravity. It contravenes every purpose of religion, and defeats every object for which the Church was brought into existence. If slavery could have a place in the Church, religion would be an idle delusion — a grotesque absurdity. A reformatory and humanizing institution that should tolerate the worst possible despotism, and

an aggregation of the greatest crimes ever committed would deserve the scorn and contempt of mankind — if, indeed, it were not beneath contempt.

None of the apologies offered in extenuation of religious slave-holding have any weight. They are only bad excuses for a bad cause. The favorite plea of mercy we have exploded, as a most unfounded abuse of terms. There can be no mercy in slave-holding. Besides the plea, if not wanting in sincerity and honesty, is utterly fallacious. Christian slave-holders do not change the nature of the business at all. Their slaves are still chattels—still subject to the laws of property — still unable to marry or to own property, or to obtain an education, or to serve God. Slavery is slavery, whether in the Church or out of it. It is a crushing despotism, which the Christian is equally unable either to endure himself, or inflict on others. It is a vile abuse, as repugnant to Christianity as any other crime peculiar to the most debased heathen nations. The idea of adopting it into the Church, is an extravagance of error — a madness and desperation of purpose that has no parallel. Happily for the reputation of Christianity, its benign principles are too well known to suffer materially from these attempts to link its destiny with this rank and enduring off-shoot of pagan *cruelty*. A system which teaches that man was made in the image of God — made to be holy and happy — is grossly slandered when represented as patronizing such a shameless crime as slavery.

PART III.

DUTY OF THE CHURCH IN RELATION TO SLAVERY.

CHAPTER I.

EXTIRPATION OF SLAVERY FROM THE CHURCH.

HAVING affirmed, and, as we believe, demonstrated that "slavery is a sin, a great sin, and a sin under all circumstances," it would be somewhat worse than idle to affect any difficulty in determining the duty of the Church towards it. What the duty of the Church is in relation to crime, can never be doubtful. Even slave-holders have no doubt here. Their controversy is solely with the premises — not with the conclusion to which we arrive. If slavery is a sin necessarily subversive of Christian character, no one — not even the most guilty offender — can object to its immediate exclusion from the Church. The duty of the Church is precisely the same towards all the varied catalogue of crimes — renunciation and exclusion are the only lawful treatment that can possibly be accorded to them. So far as the slave-holder is concerned, the treatment due is the same as that which is due to the adulterer or the thief, the burglar or the murderer. But, by the extirpation of slavery, we mean still more. It is not enough that slave-holders be expelled; the man who consents to be a slave equally deserves expulsion. He had no right to yield himself to human authority, to the exclusion of the authority of God; nor had he any right to part with endowments and faculties which the Creator had bestowed upon him as a human being, and take a station among the brutes. The man or woman who will do this is not prepared for Church membership, and should not be permitted to assume obligations, the fulfillment of which is rendered impossible. The Church requires chastity in its members, but how can the female be chaste when she relinquishes the right to control her own conduct, and becomes subject to her master, or to any whom he may appoint, in all things? If her owner insists upon defiling her, it is unquestionably her duty as a slave to submit, and if she does not submit, the master can inflict what punishment he pleases — if she resists with becoming spirit, he is authorized to kill her at once. The Church requires parents to take care of their children, but how can slave parents do this, when their children are taken from them and sold to the slave trader? Thus we might specify all the varied duties exacted by the Church, and slavery would be found to render them impracticable. For this reason, no slave should be allowed in the Church. Unless persons can throw off the shackles of bondage far enough to be Christ's freemen, it is a sad perversion, to devolve upon them the responsibilities of Christianity. If they are to be kept degraded to the condition of brutes, nothing unsuitable for brutes should be exacted of them. Christianity was designed for human beings, and we must bring the slave up to this, his natural position, or deny him a place in the Church. It would be deemed a profanation to take horses and cattle into the Church, but if we reduce men to the same condition, they become equally unfit for Church relations.

Slavery, it is true, is only factitiously and outwardly in the Church. But this merely external connection is reprehensible, and ought to be repudiated. It is a great scandal that so vile a sin is allowed even a nominal relation to a body professing holiness. Either slavery should be put down, or all sin should be tolerated. Few will object to this 'position, provided we have reference only to the worst kind of slave-holders, and the most besotted of slaves. It is conceded that these are not Christians, and, therefore, ought not to be Church members. But, it is insisted that many are involuntary slave-holders and slaves, and by consequence, not chargeable with the guilt so evidently resting upon others. A satisfactory reply to this allegation is at hand. Do we excuse men from the commission of crimes merely because they suffered themselves to be enticed into them? Is the man who involuntarily gets drunk, or involuntarily kills another, excusable? Never — unless he did all in his power to prevent such acts. He may be less guilty, perhaps, than if he had deliberately planned and executed these crimes, but he is guilty of not controlling his powers. The will is ours, and we are responsible for its exercise; but not the will alone. It is the province of the will to regulate the other powers, and keep them from sin; if it does not effect this, the individual is pronounced to be guilty—his involuntariness is no exculpation. A man must not lend himself as an instrument for others to use in the accomplishment of purposes which his own judgment and conscience condemn. These involuntary slaves and slave-holders are, therefore, guilty; they have not resisted an odious system, but have allowed it to draw them into crime.

It has been said that non-slave-holding is, in many instances, utterly impossible — that a man may have slaves left him by will, and without his knowledge or consent. This is simply a fallacy. No man can be a slave-holder, any more than he can be a murderer, without his knowledge or consent. Slave property may be devolved upon any man, but that does not oblige him to accept it. He can refuse to acknowledge or treat such persons as his slaves — can set them at liberty, or leave them to be disposed of by others, as the law may direct. He is no more obliged to own slaves contrary to his will, than he is to own any other kind of property. Until the man accepts the property as his own, and receives it in the character which the law gives to it, he is not a slave-holder in the proper sense of the word. The same is true of the slave. No man is a slave, merely because the law pronounces him such. He can only be a slave by the actual enforcement of the law. The law is naught to him until it takes effect, and strikes him from among men. This may be prevented by that stubborn resistance with which every human being is bound to meet enactments that contravene the laws of God.

But if slavery is to be extirpated from the Church, there must be a rule to this effect. Many sins are so well known, and their character so little in dispute, that ecclesiastical legislation is unnecessary : nothing is wanted but action. No Church presumes to enact a rule against robbery or murder, and yet all Churches promptly expel members thus offending. Were slavery fully understood, a Church law prohibiting it would be equally useless. At present, we need an express prohibitory statute in the Church, in order to secure action. The moral sense of community is not sufficiently developed in this direction, to effect the removal of the guilty without some provision of this kind. With such a law embodied in Church discipline as expressive of the sense of the membership, the administration could go on with due regard to all exceptional cases. It might be found, occasionally, as is often the case in other instances of alleged crime, that the offence was only nominal. Thus the truly innocent would be acquitted, while the guilty were condemned, to the great relief of the Church. Until slave-holding, under all possible circumstances, is regarded as a crime, and so defined upon the statutory records of the Church, we shall see no reform in this matter. Without a specific rule, there is no way of

reaching any enormity practiced under the slave code.
The master, being permitted to hold slaves, must, of
course, be permitted to hold them as other men do —
that is to say, he must be allowed to execute the slave
law in all its details.   He cannot be expected to oppress men without availing himself of oppressive
laws.   But if slavery is outlawed, and declared to be
incompatible with Church relations, the Church then
becomes judge in the case, and merely nominal slave-
holding, if any such there be, will appear in its true
character.   As things are at present, slavery is sanctioned by not being condemned.   The absence of law
against it, proves that toleration was intended.   And
if, in given cases, slave-holding is rendered merely
nominal by the force of those elevated precepts which
Christianity inculcates, the Church gains no credit,
and deserves none, because she did not prohibit an
evil so clearly repugnant to the principles of religion.
If slavery is modified and reformed so as to comport,
in any degree, with humanity, it is purely accidental.
The Church has made no provision for such a result.
Slave-holders are left to do as they please; they riot in
unbounded liberty, and will continue to do so while
slavery is tolerated.   The sum is this : Slavery is sin,
and the Church, following the word of God, condemns
all sin, but yet does not specifically condemn slavery.
This, as we have said, would be no detriment, were
slavery fully understood and promptly repelled, as
are other great sins ; but it is not, and the only remedy is to enact a prohibitory rule.

CHAPTER II.

EXTIRPATION OF SLAVERY FROM THE WORLD.

THE influence of the Church should extend far beyond its own communion. When ecclesiastical rules are right, and rightly administered, their effect cannot be limited to the Church alone; it will be felt in the world, and will powerfully contribute to the subversion of every species of wickedness. The Church must be the assailant of all sin, and not merely of that which is within its own pale. Its mission is to establish the kingdom of God on earth by the banishment of unrighteousness, and the introduction of universal holiness.

But as slavery, though sinful, is a legal institution, it is claimed by some that the Church cannot oppose it without improperly descending to secular strife; and above all, it is claimed that such an opposition would be an unlawful interference with the functions of civil government. The absurdity of these objections we shall briefly expose.

That piety which overlooks crime under a pretence of refined or elevated spirituality, is of a very suspicious character. Pharisaism and Jesuitism, in their murderous, diabolical career, have never been wanting in precisely this kind of discrimination. They have set at naught all principles of justice and humanity for the avowed purpose of carrying religion forward by other than the usual methods, or of uniting it with character in the absence of practical morality. Thus, while they were planning assassinations and robberies, committing adulteries and perjuries, wallowing in all the debasement of Machiavelian intrigues — they were models of devoutness, and pillars of the Church. Such spiritualism must not be mistaken for religion. It is a morbid, hypocritical piety, and worthy of the deepest abhorrence. And it is so mainly for the reason that the common duties of life are divorced. Those ordinary and lesser virtues peculiar to social, every-day life — those duties which man owes to man — are eschewed, and in place of them, we have nothing but blind devotion to the Church. These are characters trained for the Church as a system, and bound to build it up regardless of religious obligation. Forgetting the first principles of the religion they profess, and devoting themselves wholly to Church extension, they vainly attempt to build up the cause of God by trampling his own holy precepts under their feet. This is done for the Church! They compass sea and land to make proselytes, and those proselytes, when made, are only so much the more children of hell. Yet this is the inevitable effect of all attempts to propagate religion by neglecting rigid attention to all kinds of practical morality. If, for the sake of extending the Church, or keeping it free from secular contamination, we pass over as unworthy of notice, the cruel injustice inflicted by slavery, the effect will be, not spirituality, but the reverse — carnality and death. The Church cannot wink at these

wrongs and keep herself pure.   It is the business of
the Church to teach men their duty in all the relations of life.   To pass by temporal affairs, and overlook minor duties, with a view to higher interests, is
quite consistent with the gospel, provided no real injustice be done.   But we must not leave men in
deadly sins, we must not sanction vice in our efforts
to teach virtue, nor kill the body to preserve the soul.
Here is where this description of religious propa-
gandists signally fail.   They incorporate the precious
with the vile ; they sanctify the sin of slavery, and
give it a place in the Church, rather than encounter
the opposition of slave-holders.

2. The conflict with civil law, where such law is
corrupt, is absolutely unavoidable.   But still, it is
said, "we have nothing to do with government.
Slavery is the creature of law, and we must obey the
powers that be."   All this may be very convenient
for Jesuitical purposes, but no Christian can, for a
moment, tolerate such a sentiment.   Suppose the civil
law should prohibit the worship of God.   Would it
not be our duty to oppose the law even unto death ?
None can deny that it would.   How, then, can it be
said that we have nothing to do with government but
to submit implicitly to its requirements ?   If we may
resist goverment in one case, we may in another,
provided both are equally wrong.   Hence there is
no way to make the authority of the civil law any
apology for slavery, but by supposing that the law is
right.   We must take for granted that slavery is not
a sin, and that the law is right because it exacts no-

thing wrong. On no other principle can a refusal to interfere with the law, be justified. Unfortunately, however, those who plead the authority of law, acknowledge that slavery is wrong. They do not perceive the fatal character of this admission; surely, they are not ready to do all the wrongs that law might possibly enjoin, but are contented to do this wrong. If they would reflect for a moment, it could not escape them that the law had no more authority to uphold slavery than it has to uphold any or all other crimes.

Let it be remembered that all the martyrs were the victims of unrighteous civil law. They bled because they would not violate their consciences by obeying man rather than God. It was not enough for them to know that human government required certain things—" they confessed that they were pilgrims and strangers on earth," and consequently, that the law of God was supreme over them, and utterly forbid their doing wrong, no matter who might command to the contrary.

That slavery is established by law, we must admit; but this does not, in the least, prove its innocence. Laws often ordain vice as well as virtue, and the Christian who attempts to do all that the civil law allows, will often find himself grossly at variance with the gospel of Christ. The law of God enjoins holiness, and all human laws which either command or tolerate wickedness, are not only of no authority, but deserve to be rejected with abhorrence. Happily the slave law is only permissive; no man is required to hold slaves.   It is, therefore, evidence of something worse than blind reverence for civil law, when Christians condescend to the practice of slavery.   It shows a love for slave-holding — a proclivity for crime which gladly seeks shelter under the umbrage of human authority.   This is the more evident, as the same class of persons who are so remarkably reverent towards the civil law wherein it establishes slavery, have no hesitation in opposing the same law in other respects. If the government should trample upon their rights in any respect they would not withhold the most indignant remonstrance.   But when the usurpation is in their favor — when the law gives the colored man's services to them for little or nothing, and makes him an article of property, then they bow to law with strange precision, and preach against all resistance of the horrible statute.   When the advocates of slavery, and of this passive, indiscriminate submission to human government, are ready to become slaves themselves, or to obey the law in all things, however palpable its wickedness, then we may count them sincere, if not wise.

CHAPTER III.

THE EXCLUSION OF SLAVERY DEMANDED BY AN IMPARTIAL ADMINISTRATION OF CHURCH DISCIPLINE.

THERE are many sins not named either in the Bible or in the canons of the Church, for which men are excluded. It avails nothing, therefore, that slavery is not specifically prohibited. The general rule in all Churches is, *holiness in all things*. This rule abundantly justifies the exclusion of everything sinful, whether specified or not. As Church discipline is now administered, it takes effect only in particular cases. The robber meets with exemplary punishment, and so do the extortioner and the thief — that is, they meet with punishment when these acts occur apart from slavery. But when the slave law sanctions the robbery, the theft, and the extortion, all combined, and carried to such an extent as they are never carried by the professional bandit, the deed is passed over in silence. In the case of adultery, or criminal intercourse of the sexes, we have a still more striking instance of injustice. These crimes are rigidly excluded from all orthodox Churches, except as slavery introduces them. Slaves not being permitted to marry, must of necessity live together without marriage. Hence the Church tolerates this unlawful commerce of the sexes among slaves, as she does not among others. There is no application of discipline to slavery,

in this respect. Promiscuous, unbounded licentiousness exists without any possible check. The Church
may repeat its form of marriage over the slave and
his companion, but the law heeds it not, and the
parties so married are just as remorselessly sold and
separated, and polluted, as if no such ceremony had
been performed. The slave husband and wife are only such in name — the law knows them as property,
and nothing more. They live together as property,
and may be sold at any moment without the slightest
reference to the vain ceremony which pretended to
make them one forever. We question not the motives
of those who thus marry slaves, but we pronounce the
act a most egregious trifling with sacred things. Thus,
despite of all rules against concubinage, the Church
is compelled to tolerate it wherever slavery exists
within its pale. No administration can correct the
evil without removing the cause — the slave must
cease to be property before he can be married, as
marriage is affirmed only of human beings.

Besides this illicit intercourse between the sexes,
which the Church is obliged to sanction in the slave,
while she condemns it in everybody else, there is also
a necessary neglect of domestic and parental duties.
But says the apostle, " if any provide not for his own,
and especially those of his house, he hath denied the
faith, and is worse than an infidel." While the
Church generally is held strictly responsible for the
performance of this Christian duty, all slaves are
allowed to neglect it altogether, as, indeed, they ever
must be. The slave has nothing, and can acquire

nothing; his family—so called—are, therefore, wholly dependent upon others, and the law which applies to all other members of the Church, becomes inoperative upon him. The Church can do no better than to pass him by, while she allows the slave-holder to claim both his body and soul as chattels personal. But the lack of providing for a family in mere temporalities, is not the worst — the offspring of this universal concubinage must grow up without parental control or care. The parents cannot fulfill even the most obvious duties towards their children. The master has the only real authority, and whatever may be the design or wishes of the parents touching the regulation of their children, nothing is practicable but at the instance of the proprietor. And as it is for his interest to have all slave-children kept in ignorance, that they may with greater convenience be kept slaves, cultivation is out of the question. The parents are powerless; and the owner having no design but to degrade, the Church is obliged to witness the slave-growing process in all its stages — nay, more, is obliged to be the patron and approver of the abomination. Discipline there cannot be in the case, for the slave is surrendered to just the fate which is thus meted out to him. In consenting to tolerate slavery in the Church, we give our sanction to all the degradation necessary to keep the institution unimpaired. The slave-breeders of Virginia and Maryland who stock the Southern market, have Church authority for their infernal business. The children whom they thus raise and sell, were permitted to grow up just as other slaves are, that is, fitted for slavery. Were the Church to object to this rearing of slaves; were she to insist that no child should be kept degraded in this horrible manner, the institution of slavery would soon be at an end.

It is almost equally impossible to administer discipline among the slave-holders themselves, even setting aside the immorality of slavery itself. As slaves are not allowed to be witnesses in any case against a white person, the slave-holder may practice any enormity without the slightest danger of expulsion from the Church, unless some one besides slaves can be brought to testify against him. Wrongs inflicted on slaves, a class peculiarly exposed to every species of abuse, are, of course, seldom actionable. No cruelty, or debauchery, or profanity, or falsehood towards a slave, has any reasonable chance of correction. It is easy to practice the greatest crimes, and keep them forever out of the reach, if not out of the knowledge, of the Church. Slave-holding Church members, therefore, constitute an exception to all rules of morality, and to all Church discipline. They are left to do as they please with their slaves, save when others than slaves are present. None but slave-holders ever had such indulgence, and it is not possible that ecclesiastical discipline should be much better than a farce, while crippled in this extraordinary manner.

But we will not insist on minor objections. The grand reason for the abolition of slavery in the Church is, that without it no sufficient standard of purity can ever be attained. The acts of other men are subjected to careful supervision, and visited with appropriate censure; but the slave-holder escapes uncensured. His conduct must pass without inspection. Though slavery is "the sum of all villanies," it may not be investigated and adjudged like other crimes. It is at once classed among venial faults, and the Church covers it with a mantle of charity. Justice demands that slavery be analyzed and classified — that its essential character shall be its justification. Now it stands upon prescription, and though marked in every part with the greatest atrocities, no censure is inflicted, because the institution is uncondemned. The slave-holder may steal all that a man has, and the man himself, but it is no sin, and the Church is quiescent. But let the non-slave-holder pilfer even a single shilling, and he is promptly excluded from religious society. Is this impartial? Is it equitable to punish severely the less guilty, while the greatest culprits are allowed to escape with impunity?

The Church legislates in vain against the peccadilloes of its non-slave-holding members, while the cry of the oppressed is suffered to pass unheeded. It is impossible to establish virtue in communities where the greatest crimes are either openly or secretly abetted; the most that can be attained, under such circumstances, is to follow in the steps of the Pharisees, who paid tithes "of mint and rue, and passed over judgment and the love of God." Nothing but the externals of religion, can have any existence in the heart or life until all sin is put away. Let slavery be made an exception because the law wills it or the people desire it, and all evangelical influence is at an end. We might as well seek to unite piety with blasphemy, as with slavery. Perhaps the religious blasphemer might be a shade more decent than the avowed infidel, but his crime would be the same in substance, and equally fatal. So the religious slave-holder may be less heartless in crushing men down to brutes, but, as he accomplishes the same result, he must incur the same guilt as the most unprincipled oppressor.

Upon the whole, neither religion nor Church discipline can be maintained in connection with this evil. The former is superficial to the last extent, and the latter is downright mockery. It is of no use to preach holiness, and countenance villany — none, whatever, to be "valiant in words," and yet so pusillanimous in deeds, as to spare the greatest atrocities. Decency requires that religion should be abandoned entirely, or else have its principles applied fairly and impartially. It is a very needless contempt of Christianity to expel men from the Church for common robbery and theft, while we retain in good standing the man-owner and man-stealer, and the trafficker in the souls and bodies of those for whom Christ shed his blood. This rottenness corrupts the Church to its centre, and sets at defiance every effort to produce moral soundness. "The whole head is sick, and the whole heart faint," and ever will be so long as slavery is tolerated. Such a vile agglomeration of the greatest crimes—such a mass of moral putrescence — cannot but carry death to everything connected with it. The Church is com-

missioned to teach not simply stern justice — the ex-
actest equity— between man and man, but to inspire
the most devoted kindness, the most tender sympathy,
and the most pure love : and if, with this high commission, it cannot elevate men above the ferocity, the
barbarism, the wanton cruelty, and the immeasurable
injustice of slavery, we may pronounce its claims as
a reformatory agent, utterly unfounded.   If it cannot
or will not correct so palpable a wrong as slavery, it
cannot, with decency, assume to improve the morals
of mankind in any respect.   It is out of all character
to teach honesty and connive at dishonesty — nay,
worse, to teach honesty in minor things, and teach
dishonesty in things of the highest consequence.
Such perverseness may ally itself with the mere form
of religion, and may consist, perhaps, with the sem-
blance of ecclesiastical discipline ; but it can never
have place in the true Church, nor abide for a moment a righteous administration.   Slavery is a moun-
tain of guilt that must sink down before the order
of the Church can be observed ; and were there no
word in all the Bible against it — were the several
crimes of which it is but the aggregate, unnamed —
still the duty of cultivating purity would necessarily
array every Christian in eternal hostility to an institution so contemptible in spirit, and so debasing in
practice.

CHAPTER IV.

THE EXCLUSION OF SLAVERY ESSENTIAL TO THE PEACE AND UNITY OF THE CHURCH.

It is believed by many that all discussion on the subject of slavery, and especially all attempts to exclude slavery from the Church, are subversive of peace, and productive of secession. That these apprehensions are wholly unfounded, is quite evident. But unfounded as they are, they have been industriously used to bring into discredit every effort to discuss the question of slavery. Those who would not be silent, have been charged as disturbers of the peace of Zion — as ambitious aspirants and reckless disunionists. The Church is supposed to be endangered and ready to fall to pieces, whenever the subject of slavery is mentioned. Against these idle fears, and these unjust imputations, we enter our protest.

Secession is always possible, inasmuch as men may secede with or without cause, there being no law that can keep them in the Church, contrary to their wishes. But the bare possibility of secession does not prove even its probability, much less its necessity. Why, then, the cry of secession? It looks to us like attempting to break down the inquiry by an approbrious suggestion — as though investigation would be defeat, and the discussion must be stifled by connecting it with something odious. This is a common, but not very profound way of carrying a point, where the cause is bad and cannot be sustained by fair means. To give a man a bad name, will often injure him with the public, or exasperate him; the first leads to discouragement, the second to indiscretion. This early, wide-spread noise about secession, may not have been designed to forestall public opinion, but whether designed or not, its effect will naturally be the same. It is a very cheap mode of warfare — it requires neither learning nor talents to call hard names, and breathe suspicion.

And can it be that there is no disposition to meet this question on its own merits? Must sober discussion be put down by the ribald cry of secession? If so, what better evidence could we have that the advocates of pro-slavery cannot maintain their ground? They are conscious of the weakness of their cause, or they never would seek to substitute vituperation for argument. We do not believe the Church will be satisfied to dispose of the subject in this way. Slavery is among us, and our relation to it is not a trivial matter, to be passed over carelessly or contemptuously. A sneer and a fling will not answer. We must have good reasons for slave-holding in the Church, or abandon it forever. If the practice can be defended by reason and Scripture, it is due to the Church that it should be so defended. But if it cannot be thus defended, the fact ought to be known, that the evil may be put away at once. It has been too much the fashion to stave off inquiry on this subject, as though things might be suffered to go on as they are, and ev-

ery effort at reform were a willful blow at the peace
of the Church. Prescription thus becomes the supreme authority. Justice, mercy and truth are set
aside, to conciliate the slave interest, and with the
vain hope of making " peace where there is no peace."
In order to this, a course of treatment such as would
not be tolerated in any other case, is continually re-
sorted to, and the trick — for it is nothing else — will,
perhaps, succeed with some, but we are confident that
the public at large will not be duped by an artifice so
exceedingly shallow.

That the slave is wronged, is a conceded fact. Why,
then, this pertinacious resistance to all inquiry into
the measure and character of his wrongs. The Church
sustains a certain relation to slavery, and if slavery
be "evil, without mixture or intermission," it illy
becomes the highest moral institution in the universe
to pass over it lightly. There ought to be deep and
prayerful scrutiny here, if anywhere, and by the
Church, if by any institution under heaven. It is
not a small matter to keep such an immense moral
evil — such a great national and individual sin —
pressed, age after age, upon the heart of the Church.
However pure the Church may be at first, it cannot
fail to become corrupted by such a foul embrace.
The loathsome vices of civil authority will surely
prove infectious, and the Church will be as the State.
Circumstances compel us to believe that the deadly
virus has already taken effect. The fear of discussion,
the naked and stupid dependence upon prescription
instead of argument, the unjust and shameless cry of

secession — are ominous of a sad decline in morals, and wholly unworthy of Christianity. Such an exhibition never takes place till a moral paralysis has supervened.

We come now to one of the main objects of this chapter, which is, to answer the following question: Has the anti-slavery movement any tendency to secession? And we hope to show that if there is such a tendency, it is, at least, not on the part of those who advocate the exclusion of slavery.

1. There is nothing in the nature of the subject to induce secession. Slavery is but a sin, and to put away sin is the professed aim of every Church regulation — it is the one work of all Church discipline. Unless it can be shown that there is something peculiarly explosive in ceasing from slavery, we can see no reason to apprehend division or alienation in any part of our work. Breaking off from this iniquity is, on the contrary, a highly conservative movement, as all holiness tends to union. Secession is fostered by vice, not by virtue; active reform is conservatism, but stolid inaction is decay and death. Again, slavery, as it exists in the Church, is either right or wrong: if right, it will surely bear investigation — it will lose nothing by the most rigid inquiry; but if wrong, who would wish to cover it up? All we ask is, that the truth may come to light; that a bad practice may be condemned, or a good one approved. Is there anything preposterous or unreasonable in this? Do not candor and common honesty require that the relation of the Church to slavery should be openly and freely

examined by every one of its members? How else shall our people have a good conscience in the matter? To discuss slavery is, or should be, the same as to discuss any other question. The Christian is bound to know that what he does is right — nay, even more, that it will appear right, for he must "abstain from all appearance of evil." He may not plead custom, he is not privileged to do as others do, but is under the most solemn obligations to know that his acts are conformed to the law of God.

2. Neither is there anything in discussion itself to cause secession. Men may examine questions of morality and duty without the least offence, and with great profit, as is proved by every evangelical volume or sermon given to the world. It is not bare discussion of religious subjects that produces evil, else we must cease from all doctrinal investigations — we must neither refute heresy nor vindicate truth. If evil arises, then, it can only come from the manner of conducting the controversy. An angry, uncharitable, supercilious debate would be injurious, because these tempers are in themselves an evil, and can only lead to evil. But there is not the least necessity for the indulgence of such dispositions. They are as unsuitable and foreign to this as to all other grave and important subjects of inquiry; they have no more intimate connection with slavery than with drunkenness and avarice. Guilt, however, dreads exposure, and an irrascible temper, in those who plead for slave-holding in the Church, has too often borne stronger testimony against the practice than all the arguments of

its opponents. A feverish anxiety to suppress all debate, and a sensitiveness that rushes to desperation at
the very mention of change, are indications not to be
mistaken. "Every one that doeth evil hateth the
light, neither cometh to the light, lest his deeds should
be reproved." Those who are confident of the rectitude of their principles and practices, always invite
scrutiny — they challenge that investigation which
all who have not this confidence so much dread. It
is evident, therefore, that the searchings of the present anti-slavery movement will not disturb any who
should not be disturbed. The inquiry must be grate-
ful to those who think themselves unjustly accused,
and troublesome only to such as dare not come to the
light. It will tend to union, and not to disunion.

3. The condition of those engaged in the movement
is not such as to invite secession. Disappointed aspirants, idle speculatists, and visionary enthusiasts are
one thing; cool, determined, practical men are another. There is no excitement, no disaffection, no
haste; the movement is one of sober second thought.
It is an honest and frank declaration of sentiment,
accompanied by a firm determination to support the
declaration by corresponding action. But if those
who believe slave-holding should not be tolerated in
the Church, cannot effect an amendment in this particular, they have sense enough, we trust, to know
that time and perseverance are requisite in all great
undertakings. Should they fail now, they will succeed hereafter, and can afford to wait. Men who are
in a hurry are not fitted for great achievements. Re-

form is a life work; it is not the accident of a day, but the patient, unwavering effort of a whole existence. That men of unflinching firmness and subdued expectation, of clear perception and moral force, will think it wise to leave the Church for this cause, we do not believe. Secession is too extreme a remedy for such a disease. The very mention of it is an insult. It implies that men do not know enough to desire and labor for an object without bolting from the Church, in case of failure. We despise secession, where the liberty of working is allowed. It is downright folly; for once out of the Church, all hope of benefiting it is at an end. Nothing would please the slave-holder better than to have those opposed to him leave the Church; he could then have it all his own way. Besides, we are not for deserting the sick. Slavery is a moral disease, and while it preys upon the vitals of the Church, we ought to be peculiarly devoted and unshrinking in our attachment. A friend should never be forsaken in the hour of need.

4. Secession must have a motive, but there is no possible motive in this case. We have just as much liberty to oppose slavery in the Church, as we could have out of it. There is no restriction whatever. The Church meditates unsparing opposition, and invites us to it. The Methodist Episcopal Church, in particular, asks, " What shall be done for the extirpation of the evil of slavery ?" and bids us respond. Shall we meanly shrink from the work solicited at our hands ? Shall we abscond in the hour of peril and of action ? Did Luther forsake the Catholic Church, or

did that Church forsake him? The latter. Did Wesley forsake the English Church? Never. Both had other work to do. They hazarded life to restore the fallen — they labored long and arduously to build up the waste places, the "desolations of many generations." So should every reformer do, and only cease from his Church relations when he ceases from life. To dash out of the Church is a foolish expedient; it has been the ruin of many a well begun work.

5. It is not a little ridiculous to suppose that a calm, fraternal discussion must end in the convulsive throes of ecclesiastical dissolution. Freedom of speech is essential to liberty in Church and State. Corruption and tyranny invoke silence, but truth and righteousness invite utterance. The latter have nothing to conceal — nothing that they do not wish to have circulated to the remotest extent. But tyranny claims to rule without a reason; it maddens at the thought of inquiry, and exacts a blind and brutal submission. The idea that this free expression, so harmless and so necessary to religion, is dangerous, is an unmatched absurdity. It is to mistake the best friend of religion for its greatest enemy. The blood in our veins is not more important to the health of the body, than free speech in our mouths is to the health of the Church.

Let no one, therefore, agonize over the dangers of discussion. It is to borrow trouble from what should be our greatest consolation. Where is liberty in the State, or purity in the Church, at this moment? Is it in Italy or Russia, where freedom of speech is unknown? or is it in England and the United States, where men write and speak as they please? If we wish for the midnight of error and corruption, then let us declaim against investigation.

We shall now show more directly that the extirpation of slavery is not only safe, but every way conducive to the peace and unity of the Church.

1. Slavery is sin — so conceded to be, even by the most of those who plead for its continuance in the Church — and sin is the cause of all disturbances and divisions in the Church. If, therefore, we can remove the cause, the effect will cease. Unity and peace are ever in proportion to holiness. To put away sin is to produce union, not to destroy it. Hence, in assuming that the extirpation of slavery will occasion secession, we also assume that slavery is a pure institution. But, in spite of this unavoidable inference, we are met with the objection that the tares and the wheat must grow together, lest, in pulling up one, we pull up the other also. But this construction of the parable of the tares and the wheat, is by no means tenable. If good here, it is good everywhere, and the consequence will be that no sinner, however great his crimes, can be expelled from the Church. Drunkards and adulterers, murderers and blasphemers, must be retained as well as slave-holders. Such an interpretation arrays the Bible against itself, and makes the existing usage of all Churches — for all Churches exclude murderers and blasphemers — unjustifiable oppression. Moreover, the passage cannot be so

construed without palpably contradicting the exposition given by Christ in the subsequent verses of the chapter. "He that soweth the good seed is the Son of man ; the field is the world ; the good seed are the children of the kingdom ; but the tares are the children of the wicked one ; the enemy that sowed them is the devil ; the harvest is the end of the world, and the reapers are the angels." (*Matt.* xiii, 38.) It is plain enough that the caution was not against excluding flagrant sinners, or "the children of the wicked one" from the Church, but against exterminating them from the world. The field is the whole world, not simply the Church. Whitby's note on this parable is remarkably just :

"Some collect that even the tares must be members of the Church of Christ, as well as the good seed, which, if it only signify they by profession may be so, is in itself true ; but if it be designed to prove that they are true members of that body, of which Jesus Christ is the head, that cannot follow from these words : for 1, our Savior saith expressly, 'the field is' not the Church, but 'the world.' 2. The seed sown in the field by Christ is good seed, 'the children of the kingdom,' (*ver.* 38,) 'the just', (*ver.* 43 ;) they, therefore, only can belong to him, because they only are sown by him ; the tares were sown in it by the envious man, that is the devil, (*ver.* 28,) the enemy of Christ and the Church ; they are sown while the overseers of the Church were asleep, and are expressly called 'the children of the devil.' And is it reasonable to conceive that the devil, the great enemy of the Church and of its head, should beget members to his Church, since 'there is no communion betwixt Christ and Belial,' or that the devil's children should be members of Christ's body ? Vain hence is the collection [inference] of the Erastians, that the wicked, and those that cause offences, are not by excommunication to be excluded from the communion of the Church, seeing the field in which the tares spring up is not the Church, but the world."

2. Slave-holders may complain, and doubtless will, of any effort to separate them or their practices from the Church, but as they are not of the Church in any proper sense, it will not disturb the peace of Christians; and if all slave-holders secede, instead of reforming, they will go out of the Church only because they are not of it — there will be no loss. The exclusion of such can have no other than a salutary effect. Unless it can be shown that corruption is necessary to purity — that a diseased limb promotes the health of the rest of the body — that contagion is prevented by pestilence — we can see no reason why the extirpation of the evil of slavery should not greatly promote the welfare of the Church. Something in point of numbers would perhaps be lost, but that loss would be an unspeakable gain. While it subtracted nothing from the life of the Church, it would remove a dead weight — a useless, putrescent incumbrance — as dangerous as it is unsightly and loathsome.

3. Slavery impairs the discipline of the Church, and thus paves the road to ruin. We have seen that no faithful, impartial application of Church discipline is possible where slavery obtains. Neither master nor slave can be required to do what God has enjoined upon every Christian. In this case a gradual deterioration must supervene. Where the morals of the Church are left to chance, or to an inefficient super-

vision, the worst corruptions cannot be long delayed. The master is allowed to do what is wrong, but this is not all; for even those crimes which are prohibited, escape censure, because slaves are not permitted to be witnesses. This restriction of testimony is enough to sap the foundation of any Church. But the slave is almost wholly beyond the reach of Church regulations. No relief can be brought to him from this source. Church member though he be, education, marriage, parental authority, self-government, and freedom are as far from him as if no Church existed on earth. Now these imbruted beings, so far as they have a nominal or real connection with religion, must certainly be every way improved by emancipation. As they are at present, the Church has little to do with them; the rending of their chains might bring them up to Christian privileges, but it could not possibly deprive them of such privileges, for they never had them, and never can have them as slaves. The Church occupies a feeble, trembling existence — if it exists at all — in connection with slavery, and the whole effect of abolishing slavery would be beneficial in the highest degree.

4. Slavery impairs the morals of the Church, and therefore puts it in continual jeopardy. A low state of religion is necessarily fruitful of discord and strife. It is the pure who dwell together in unity. The history of Church divisions would show that they have invariably proceeded from a lack of moral principle. But nothing could more effectually blunt all perception of right and wrong than an institution which at one

sweep strikes down to the dust innocent men, together with their wives and children. This enormous, unprovoked offence, if allowed to pass without censure, opens the way to fathomless corruption. It is the fitting precursor of any subsequent villanies that the most shameless depravity can suggest. Where the moral sense of the Church must be kept so obtuse as to acquiesce in the " sum of all villanies," other and lesser evils will of course follow in due time. The canker of unrighteousness will be constantly spreading, until the whole system sickens and dies. With moral perceptions deadened sufficiently to endure such arrant wickedness, no community can long sustain more than the form of religion. Hence, to abolish slavery is an indispensable condition of religious prosperity.

5. Slavery impedes the progress of the Church. The religious culture of slaves must be exceedingly limited, and that of their masters not less so. The latter, it is true, may be taught to read, and may, without mockery, be instructed in the duties of conjugal, parental, and filial relations, but who shall teach them to let the oppressed go free ? Who shall teach them to do to others as they would that others should do unto them, and yet not subvert slavery ? This necessity of inculcating all holiness, and still leaving untouched one of the grossest crimes ever committed by man against his fellow man, obliges the Church to invent apologies for slave-holding, and to enter upon a course of extenuation where reproof and conviction were needed. In such a community, reform can pro-

7*

ceed only to a certain extent; if the axe is laid at the
root of the tree, the system of slavery perishes at once.
Here, then, is a source of perpetual irritation and defeat. Every effort to extend the work of reformation
recoils upon itself, or else attacks the vitality of slavery. Can the Church prosper when its onward march
is thus interrupted — when it marshals its forces for
the onset, and is compelled to disband them without
striking a blow?

6. But the grand reason is yet to be named. Religion and slavery are utterly and eternally hostile to
each other. They cannot be reconciled, and all attempts to reconcile them are worse than useless. Virtue and vice have no affinity. Consequently, so long
as slavery is in the Church in any shape or degree, it
must be the occasion of an exterminating warfare.
Good men must hate sin, and, hating it, must always
aim at excluding it from the Church and the world.
As well might we hope to make fire and water coa-
lesce — as well blend light with darkness, or the summer's heat with the winter's cold. What one gains,
the other loses; just as slavery is spared, the Church
is depreciated. It is this antagonism that makes the
abolition of slavery so essential to the peace and unity
of the Church. The pure are so constituted that they
cannot and will not fellowship sin; and while sin is
tolerated in the Church, there must inevitably be con-
tention, if not disruption. A burning, incorruptible
holiness will loathe and abominate such filthiness of
flesh and spirit as is engendered by the slave code;
nor can prudential considerations, whether of civil or

ecclesiastical origin, long hold the rampant hatred in
check.   Men may " cry peace, but there is no peace."
There never can be peace between sin and holiness.
In vain are all expedients to unite what God has put
asunder forever.   It is this unavoidable collision of
hostile elements that renders every effort to gloss
slavery and incorporate it with the Church so perfect-
ly futile.   The effort cannot be successful ; but if it
could, the result would be interminable strife — it
would be to fasten upon the Church chaotic ruin and
unmatched anarchy to the latest hour of time.   Chained
to the dead body of slavery, the living Church could
only drag out a brief and sickly existence.   To prolong such a connection, whatever may be the motives,
is moral death.   The Church must die, or cast off
slavery.

CHAPTER V.

THE EXCLUSION OF SLAVERY ESSENTIAL TO THE EVAN-GELIZATION OF THE WORLD.

It has often been said, that to exclude slave-holders
from the Church would hedge up the way of mission-
aries, and prevent the progress of the gospel among
slave-holding nations.   But the objection is unfortunate — it claims too much.   We might with exactly the same propriety say, that all other legalized

iniquities shall be tolerated because an attack upon
them would embarrass the missionary. In many countries idolatry and polygamy are upheld by law as firmly
as slavery. And if we are to excuse the practice of
one of these crimes on account of the prejudice or
hostility which might arise from an effort to exclude
it from the Church, why not the other? Why not
any and all other crimes whatever? The right to
make an exception in favor of slavery, for the sake
of expediting the conversion of the slave-holder, or
securing protection to the ministry, must be broad
enough to answer in every similar instance of conflict betwixt the law of God and the law of the land.
And, yielding fully to this principle of compromise,
we should only have, on a large scale, what now occurs in lesser degree, wherever slavery is tolerated
in the Church — a religion without holiness — gospel
progress without gospel morals! On this plan, the
Church might extend itself without disturbing sin ;
the world might be converted, and yet be as wicked
as it now is. Such progress is a farce, and can never
be countenanced by any who do not wish to burlesque
Christianity.

The true state of the case is this : the gospel being
a system of holiness, cannot be allied to sin, without
destroying its own identity — it can only endorse
corruption by becoming itself corrupt. Here, then,
in the outset, arises a fatal embarrassment to all evangelical efforts. The very instrumentality that should
convert the world, is rendered powerless. But further : not only is the gospel powerless for good, and

wholly incompetent to bless the world, but it ~tually becomes one of its greatest curses. It mis ds and debases, by sanctioning and perpetuating vices which it was designed to remove. It takes away the advantages of heathen ignorance, but imparts none of the blessings of Christian knowledge. Thus the master revels in his ill-gotten gain, traffics in the souls and bodies of men, grinds to the dust those who have the same title to freedom as himself, and quotes Scripture to justify the abomination. Thus, too, the slave's natural aspirations for liberty, and all the innumerable advantages of legalized social life are blighted by a similar misapplication of the sacred writings. The Scriptures are, in fact, made to serve the purpose of chains and manacles, and the Church is converted into a slave pen. Divine authority is given to human crimes, and the gospel, instead of reforming men, only aids them in the perpetuation of crime. Such is the inevitable effect of blinking slavery in order to conciliate slave-holders, and gain access for Christianity among them.

The work of conversion is, and must be, an indiscriminate war against sin. It is not this or that evil alone that the Scriptures condemn, and from which men are to abstain, but all sin — sin of every kind and degree. Nor is there any select number of virtues that the Scriptures approve, but all virtue. The injunction is, " cease to do evil ; learn to do well." " Be ye holy." It is, therefore, impossible to preach the gospel truly and faithfully, without assailing the high-handed crime of slavery. It must be assailed in principle if not in name. And we believe there are few of the advocates for Church slavery, who do not admit that the principles of the gospel are opposed to the institution, and must, in time, subvert it wholly. They, however, strangely contend that the exclusion of slavery now is injudicious and impracticable. But they should know that lenity here is no more allowable than elsewhere. We can just as well bring people into the Church tainted with idolatry as with slavery. If the standard of religion may be lowered in one instance, it may in another, and so on till we have graduated the morals of the Church to the taste of the most depraved heathen nations. If the sin of slavery is ever to be put away, it is to be put away now. If the principles of religion condemn it at all, they condemn it now; and by condescending to retain it, we virtually say it is not safe to build the Church on its own principles. They must be held in abeyance as a matter of expediency, to facilitate the spread of religion. Such Jesuitical religion — such concealment of fundamental truths — such conniving at sin, is neither honest in itself, nor promotive of the kingdom of Christ in the earth.

If merely attacking the principle of slavery is enough, then it follows that merely attacking the principle of other vices is enough — specification and application are all unnecessary. Chastity, temperance, honesty, and faith may be taught successfully, without exciting the prejudices or correcting the practices of those who neglect these things; and if need be, the door of the Church can be opened to such, as to insist upon their reformation might lead to persecution, and hinder the spread of the gospel! This is precisely parallel with the course adopted by such as found slave-holding Churches. To avoid persecution, and to conciliate those whom they were sent to convert, they have received them into the Church, and sanctioned their errors. Should we admit to the bosom of the Church, on profession of faith, drunkards, adulterers, thieves and liars, with the full understanding that they were to renounce none of these sinful practices, our folly would not be greater, nor our efforts to evangelize the world more wretchedly disastrous than the above. It surely is no wonder that men capable of feeling the force of an argument, when pressed by such truths, are driven to deny that slavery is an intrinsic evil. They assert that it is neither good nor evil — neither right nor wrong in itself, but only made so by circumstances. This is, to all intents and purposes, a full endorsement of slavery; no slave-holder, whether professing religion or not, could, with decency, claim more. This dexterous evasion of responsibility ends at last, as might have been foreseen, not in the reformation of the slave-holder, but in the adoption of his vices by those who were commissioned to reclaim him. Such will ever be the result. As often as the Church sends out her forces to subdue the world to Christ, and makes this shameful compromise for the sake of expediting the conquest, her forces will recoil — will be beaten — will be taken captive, and arrayed against her. The sin of Achan was not more fatal to Israel at the walls of

Jericho, than the sin of slavery is to Christians in their assault upon the world, the flesh, and the devil.

There is nothing in this sin, more than in other sins, to make it exceptional. Men are as ready to relinquish slavery as they are intemperance and debauchery; they will no more despise or decapitate the minister of Christ who condemns them for this, than if he condemned them for other wrongs. But it is supposed that the civil law makes a wide difference, inasmuch as to keep slaves, special stringency is requisite, and he who declaims against the institution is a disturber of the peace, if not an insurrectionist. All this is very plausible, and may possibly happen in a given case; but it requires no great sagacity to perceive that men hold slaves as they do other wicked things. They are, therefore, approachable on the subject, and may be reasoned with, if the proper steps are taken. They are not always armed *cap a pie*, and ready for an encounter; the heart, even of the most hardened criminal, has its occasional relentings, and there are times and ways in which it is quite safe to counsel or reprove him. At least, we find no difficulty in doing this in reference to most men, and there is no good reason to believe that slavery breeds such special malignity as to render all its victims callous to reproof. Should it appear, however, that martyrdom is the only condition on which the gospel can be propagated among slave-holders, the Church will not decline the task on these terms. It will then be quite as easy as it was in apostolic times, when not only slavery but idolatry was upheld by the sword.

The first ministers went forth everywhere, and no-where had the protection of law — nowhere spared the dominant, legalized idolatry. It has been well said that " the blood of the martyrs is the seed of the Church." We are not to judge of the success of preaching solely by the favor accorded to it in the first instance. When a few have shed their blood in defence of the truth, perhaps the cause has gained more in depth and permanence than it could if they had spent their whole lives without opposition ; cer-tainly more than if they had spent them in softening the message of the Lord so as to make it agreeable to the unrenewed heart.

By extirpating slavery in the outset, the Church will stand on the only basis she can ever hope to occupy with success. She will then be seen in her true light, and cast her entire influence against all sin, making no deceptive concessions, playing no double game, and exposing herself to no corruption. Teaching men not only to amend their lives in some grosser faults, but to " perfect holiness" in the fear of the Lord, she will have the abiding presence of her invincible Head, and go forth to triumph over sla-very as she now does over other crimes. Until then her strength will not return, and she will grind in the house of her enemies.

CHAPTER VI.

THE EXCLUSION OF SLAVERY INEVITABLE.

WERE the Church disposed to compromise and retain slavery for a time, on the ground of expediency, still she has no power to do it. Every step of progress is death to slavery. The whole evangelical process, from beginning to end, subverts sin and establishes righteousness. Take, for instance, the first great truth of all religion, and especially of revealed religion, namely, the existence of God. In order to convert the slave or his master, this truth must be set forth as it is — that is to say, the true character and attributes of God must be developed to the mind of those whom we seek to convert. But here at once the master sees that human authority is not the highest, and therefore cannot be the ultimate standard of right and wrong. He sees that there may be an appeal to a higher power, and that he himself is answerable to this power. Above all, he sees that his slave has, equally with himself, the right of appeal to this higher authority. Knowing this truth, it must thenceforth be utterly impossible for him to claim ultimate or supreme authority over his slave. He will, moreover, see that the existence of such a being as God, implies rights infinitely greater than any finite being can possess ; that his slave is the creature of God, and can never belong to a fellow creature in any proper sense. The civil law may affirm one way or another, may call the slave a man or a chattel, make him the property of one or another, but he sees that God alone is, in fact, the real proprietor. Hence he can no more "lord it over God's heritage." Take, again, the doctrine of immortality. Both master and slave find that they are to live forever, and this truth not only relaxes their grasp upon the present life, so that neither can wish to do wrong by coveting or claiming what is not his own, but both have their thoughts turned to the supreme object—Heaven. Both are necessarily intent upon securing at once a full preparation for their future and eternal inheritance. This state of mind precludes slavery, because slavery precludes culture. The being who is to live forever, and whose eternal destiny depends upon an instant preparation for death, cannot be made the subject of that systematic depression peculiar to slavery. The master will be aware that the slave should have all possible facilities for moral and mental improvement — that the slave needs these helps quite as much as other men, having to prepare for the same rigorous Judgment, and the same holy Heaven. It will not be in his heart to cramp and restrict one on whom such responsibilities are devolved. He will aid the slave all in his power, and accord to him the utmost liberty that one human being can give to another. The preciousness of the soul will infinitely outweigh all temporal considerations, and virtually extinguish all power in the master to task the slave in any way, except as one Christian brother may task

another. There could be no wasting of the slave's
life and opportunities — no drudgery — no oppression,
under the influence of such a truth. But there is yet
another view of the case. The slave and his master
are to live together forever — they are co-heirs of immortality. If the master injures the slave — bruti-
fies, degrades, crushes him — the wrong will upbraid
him forever — it will stare him in the face through
eternal ages. He will spend his eternity in company
with his now slave, where " the servant is free from
his master." Can any man, with the impression that
his slave is to be elevated at death to equal privileges
with himself — to eternal glory — keep him degraded
here? Can he treat the slave as a chattel, or withhold from him any privilege that men esteem valuable? Can such a man hold a slave? We pronounce
it impossible. It is not in the nature of things that
such studied and shameless wrongs as slavery inflicts,
should be perpetrated by one who looks forward to a
beatific state, in which the slave is to be associated
with him forever, and to be an equal sharer with
himself.

But, suppose the preacher sets forth the doctrine of
holiness. He must explain the nature of sin, and especially show that it is a violation of the law of God.
He must, also, explain its fearful penalty, and bring
both the slave and his master to repentance. Now,
if there is anything wrong or sinful in slavery, it
thenceforth must cease, or the preaching is in vain.
It is only on the assumption — wholly gratuitous and
untenable — that slavery is not a moral evil, that its

longer continuance is possible.   There is just one way
of obviating this conclusion, and that is, by supposing
this sin still undiscovered — a sin of ignorance.   But
the objection would be equally valid against adultery,
robbery or murder.   As these crimes must be discovered before Christianity can make any saving progress in the soul, so must the crime of slavery — or
rather, that accumulation of crimes denominated by
the term slavery — and when discovered there is the
same imperative necessity for reformation in the one
case as in the other.   If the preacher neglects his
duty in the premises, and fails to teach that slavery
is sin, his progress in the work of evangelism will be
such as if he had neglected to teach that lying and
theft were sins against God.   He may have a Church
in form, but not in fact.

We will now leave the master out of the question
entirely, and examine yet further the effect of religious teaching upon the slave.   To make the case the
stronger, let us suppose that the missionary begins
his instruction of the slave with these words : " Servants, be obedient to them that are your masters according to the flesh."   It is not enough barely to
enunciate this passage by itself : the reason for the
injunction must be assigned, which is, that God wills
this obedience.   The slave, then, must know the comparative claims of this authority, or, in other words,
that it is higher than the authority of man.   He will
henceforth feel himself to be the subject of a new
power, and one transcendently greater than he had
before known.   But far more must follow.   With the

knowledge of that part of the gospel which we have referred to, there must be connected all the essential truths of Christianity. The slave will see that obedience to his master is not the sum of God's requirements, and not by any means an unconditional duty. He will learn that he also is a man, and has the duties of a man to perform — that a life of holiness is incumbent upon him as well as other men, and that no human authority can oblige him to sin, because God has forbidden it. He will see it his duty to be married, to take care of his wife and children, and to do all the duties which Christianity imposes upon men. This knowledge the Christian missionary is bound to communicate, and the slave is equally bound to heed it — for there is no gospel for slaves, as such, no defective messages, graduated to the limited and contingent scale of their privileges. The same glad tidings which come to other men, come to them, and must have the same purifying effect on the bond as the free. It would be mockery to make a gospel out of a few isolated precepts, as is virtually done whenever the instruction of slaves is confined to a given class of duties, or a particular set of religious truths. Such teaching may pass under the name of religion, but it deserves the severest reprobation. It is murdering the souls of men, under a pretence of saving them. Thus mutilated, the gospel becomes a powerful instrument of oppression, and is made to add its authority to the vilest enactments of the State. Taking for granted, then, what cannot be denied — that the slave must be taught to obey God rather than man, whenever human and divine requirements come into collision, we are utterly at a loss to know how any man can be a slave. It is conceded that he is a man — that, as a man, he has important rights, with which the slave code interferes — that on these rights are founded duties which must not be neglected. This being the case, we ask, how can the slave be taught that he is a man, and that the rights and duties of a man appertain to him, without being thereby incapacitated to yield those rights or neglect those duties? Why teach men that they are men, and yet compel them to relinquish the attributes of their nature? or, rather, why attempt it? — for it cannot be done. The faithful instruction of the slave is his emancipation by the act of God. He is thenceforth free in Christ, and free in the world, to all intents and purposes, save the unrighteous exactions of the civil law, which he is under the most solemn obligations to abjure and resist, whereinsoever they conflict with his duty to himself or his God.

It is admitted by many of the warmest advocates of religious slave-holding, that slavery and Christianity are inimical, and that the former must ultimately be subverted by the latter. This admission of the truth would be satisfactory, were it not for the paralyzing anachronism which attends it. Christianity will abolish slavery not only ultimately, but instantly. The work is done at once and forever. When the slave becomes a man, and assumes the responsibilities of a man — as he must under proper religious teaching — his degradation ends. He may still be a

slave in name, and the civil law may count him property only; yet he is obliged to regard himself as
God regards him — a MAN; and being a man, he must
act as a man, and not as a brute — the only character
assigned him by the slave code. We differ from those
who assert, as above stated, only in reference to the
time in which the emancipating effect of Christianity
is felt. They assume that it may be delayed; but
we affirm that delay is impossible. The emancipation is precisely coeval with the belief of God's word.
This must be, because that word involves truths respecting the slave that cannot fail to revolutionize
his conduct. Instead of regarding his owner as supreme, the moment he believes in God this supremacy is transferred, never to return. He then has a
Master in Heaven, to whom he is under_ infinitely
greater obligations than he can be to man. Like all
other believers, he may neither live nor die " to himself," nor to any created being, but only "unto the
Lord." The power of the master to dispose of him
and to control him, is dependent on the will of God,
as apprehended by the slave. He is constituted judge
of what is duty. Before him is the straight and narrow way, "which leadeth unto life," and before him,
also, is martyrdom — if need be — as the inevitable
consequence of walking in that way. But he may
not decline the path of holiness, on account of perse-
cutions — if early death must, in his case, be associated with purity, it will only give him- a brighter
crown at last.

This necessity of obeying God in all things, is not

something that arises in particular stages of religious experience, or in peculiar circumstances of life; it is, on the contrary, the one unvarying condition of all religion; there can be no saving faith where this implicit obedience is wanting. Professions and exercises there may be in any quantity, but not salvation. "Not every one that saith unto me, Lord, Lord, shall enter into the kingdom of heaven; but he that doeth the will of my Father which is in heaven." An instant obedience is demanded, and all conflicting authority is crushed as soon as the soul is affianced to its God. Over such an one the brutal slave law cannot bear sway — it must select other and more pliant material for its tyranny. Redeemed souls, who have covenanted to renounce the world, the flesh, and the devil, will not bow their necks to the God-dishonoring statutes of men.

We have, then, this single alternative — freedom or no gospel - -freedom with the gospel, or slavery without it. The law of God must extirpate the law of man, so far as the latter interferes with the requirements of the former, or the kingdom of heaven can never be established among men, nor the will of God be done in earth as it is done in heaven. It is most remarkable that any one should ever have hesitated to take this position or to make war upon human legislation in those particulars wherein it usurps the divine prerogatives, and destroys the rights of man. Such laws are clearly sinful, and ought to be — indeed, must be — resisted by all who would live unblamably. Human law is to be respected and obeyed when it is right, but in no other case ; to obey it when sinful, under the mistaken idea that we are thereby obeying God, is a manifest absurdity. All commands of this character are conditional. Human authority is good until it clashes with a higher, and then it is good for nothing. The extirpation of this form of vice — that is, legal vice — is as much incumbent upon the Christian, as is the extirpation of other forms of wickedness. Sinful legislation is to be counteracted by the preaching of the Cross, just as much when it relates to slavery as when it relates to idolatry, or Sabbath-breaking, or swindling. Or, in other words, sin is not to find a sanctuary in law. If men do wrong in making laws, the Christian is bound to overturn, if possible, those laws, and make better ones : at all events, he must not obey them. The Christian missionary is, therefore, a direct subverter of the slave law; he cannot preach without attacking it, nor be successful in his mission without breaking it down. Religion is a war against sin of every kind, and if slavery is sin, there is no alternative — it must be extirpated, or religion must cease to do its work. We have too long been deluded with the idea that Christianity has nothing to do with corrupt governments, and must make its way by Jesuitical artifices which conceal the truth or corrupt it by the adoption of error. Such a policy may answer for the spread of superstition, but it cannot promote evangelical religion. The apostles did not denounce slavery by name, nor is it necessary in all cases, but they did what is quite as effectual, they taught justice between man and man — they taught slaves that they were men, and should act like men — they enjoined all holiness upon both masters and servants — they taught all to set their affections on things above, and to remember that they had " a Master in Heaven." Now, the teaching of men thus, precluded all necessity of specifying particular sins in every instance. If we teach honesty in all things, stealing is just as effectually prohibited as it would be by a special prohibition. If we teach kindness, it is not indispensable to add a precept against cruelty and murder. The greater includes the less — positive virtue comprehends negative goodness. The apostles did not, in so many words, forbid killing a thousand men, or stealing ten thousand dollars; but as they forbade the killing of any man, and the stealing of any sum, no prohibition against these enormities was necessary. In condemning the lesser crime, they also condemned the greater. The same is true of slavery. They taught virtues and duties with which slavery is incompatible — they brought a system of kindness to bear upon a system of cruelty, a system of right upon a system of wrong, a system of holiness upon a system of sin — they let light in upon darkness, restored the slave to God and to manhood, and struck the slave law dead.

We can now see the absolute contrariety between these two systems, and the perpetual, inevitable, universal war which one must wage against the other. Christianity teaches justice, mercy, love, and truth; but slavery ignores them all in theory, and discards

them all in practice. Hence, every effort to build up
the former, must be a direct attack upon the latter.
Slavery must die just in proportion as Christianity
lives. To teach the virtues of the one, is to discoun-
tenance the vices of the other. All compromise is
out of the question, for religion can never be made to
sanction crime. The systematic oppression — the
utter contempt of all justice and humanity, by which
alone slavery is brought into existence or kept in being — is rebuked by the entire spirit of the gospel as
well as by its every precept. How, then, is it possible to propagate this religion of purity and benevolence, without, at the same time, breaking down the
corrupt and unjust system of slavery? Not to oppose
the latter, would be equivalent to suspending all the
functions of Christianity. We must cease from the
Bible, or else pervert its meaning altogether, if we
would spare the slave code. There is not a single
truth to be uttered, nor a single precept to be enforced by the minister of Christ, which does not
directly and fatally assault "the peculiar institution."
It is, therefore, impossible to retain slavery, if we
would; the Church has no option in the matter — she
cannot raise hell to heaven, nor give saintly purity to
diabolical crime. No: the constitution of the Church
excludes this foul sin, and will forever exclude it in
spite of all human authority.

CHAPTER VII.

CIVIL FREEDOM SHOULD BE MADE SUBSERVIENT TO THE CAUSE OF EMANCIPATION.

It is unquestionably the duty of the American Church, in the prosecution of its high designs, to take advantage of our republican form of government. Here the people are sovereign, not in theory only, but in fact. They make their own laws, and execute them when made. Our system of popular elections under constitutional law, effectually prevents all hereditary power, and also the accumulation of power in the hands of government functionaries. The right of the people to control and modify their form of government, and all the laws originating under it, is fully admitted. It is not esteemed disorderly, or contumacious, or unreasonable, to aim at any improvement in civil polity. So far from it, indeed, is the general sentiment of the country, and the spirit of our governmental institutions, that he who neglects to study the character of the laws, and to aid in all suitable ways the work of amendment, is justly considered as recreant to duty. It is very evident, that a Church enjoying such a form of government becomes, in part, responsible for whatever laws are enacted. This responsibility is precisely according to the measure of influence which the Church is capable of exerting on public opinion and at the polls. Knowing that slavery is oppression, and that all oppression is forbidden by God in the most pointed manner — it becomes the duty of every member of the Church to aid in the repeal of the slave law, and in the restoration of the slave to all the rights and immunities of citizenship. Even under an absolute monarchy this result would inevitably follow the propagation of Christianity, but not so speedily, nor with so little inconvenience to the Church. Such a government might not heed the wishes of Christians, however respectfully expressed; and in that case there would be no redress, save the common privilege of piety — that of laboring and suffering in conformity with the law of God, in spite of all human authority. The foundations of such a monarchy would be slowly but surely sapped by the progress of religion, and, in the end, the Church would triumph over oppression. As fast as men were converted, the government would be annihilated in all its bad features; and at last, when the number of converts was sufficiently multiplied, Christianity would assume control, as it did in the days of Constantine. Where governments are despotic, long years of suffering are requisite to accomplish ameliorations which can be reached almost at once in a republic. And since Providence has favored us, not only with a republic, but with such an one as gives to us a greater share in the regulation of civil affairs than was ever enjoyed by any other people, we are bound to make this advantage contribute to the freedom of those who are now so strangely enslaved in this land of liberty. The laws which enslave them are, in no inconsiderable degree, dependent for their character and stability on the action of the Church. If the Church condemns these laws, and faithfully labors to subvert them, they must soon yield to an improved legislation. But if she passes them by as unworthy of notice, or as evils, the correction of which is altogether beyond her province, the now dominant, unrebuked, but wicked legislation, which originated these laws, will probably be able to enforce them yet longer.

The fact that Christians in the apostolic age had little or no political influence, and were not at all consulted in the enactment of laws, does not, by itself, account for the manner in which the subject of slavery was treated by the apostles. They contented themselves with saying, " Be not ye the servants of men." They said to all, " Be ye holy." This obligation to do no wrong, and to " abstain from all appearance of evil," was a death blow to slavery ; it comprehended much more than merely emancipating the slave, as it bound the master as well as the slave to a life of reciprocal charity — made them brethren of the same family, and heirs together of the grace of God. Thus the apostles did not refrain from direct political teaching, though they couched their instructions on the subject in general terms. The command to be holy is just as positive and direct a prohibition of murder as is the injunction, " thou shalt not kill." It has been supposed that the apostles were mainly silent on political subjects, and that the limited power of the Church in matters of civil government was the occasion of this silence. But we contend they were not silent. By prohibiting all sin, they have as effectually condemned the sin of slavery as it was possible for words to do. No concession can be made here, for if the apostles shunned political questions on the above ground, there is no good reason why they should have confined their caution to slavery. Christians were just as powerless in reference to other political grievances. The law upheld idolatry, and the same prudence which dictated silence in reference to slavery, should have prevented all mention of idol-worship. The truth is, slavery became an impossibility under the gospel dispensation. It could not live a moment in the kingdom of God. It was condemned by every precept and spurned by every truth in the gospel message. Hence, there was no more need of particularizing it among things prohibited, than there was of particularizing cannibalism. Minuteness of specification here would have been out of place. As teachers of supernatural and immaculate holiness, it did not become the apostles to waste words on so gross a complication of villanies. After enjoining all kindness and brotherly love, it could not be expected that they would specifically inhibit the grossest brutalities. We therefore have no difficulty in accounting for any absence of formal prohibitions against slavery. It is not necessary to find reasons for apostolic silence, since that silence does not exist. Every command was a prohibition in fact, and every prohibition was as plain as language could make it.

It should be observed, that our democratic form of

government opens every question of law to public discussion. This is true even in the slave States. The constitutions of those States are subject to revision whenever the people choose, and nothing more is requisite to effect any legal reform than simply to change the state of public sentiment. Churches situated in slave-holding States have nothing to do but avail themselves of their acknowledged political rights. In the exercise of these rights, they can soon restore the slave to manhood, and blot out every slave law from the statute book.

As yet, anti-slavery principles have flourished most in the free States, and for the best of reasons ; though some have deemed all agitation of the subject, except on slave territory, quite out of place. But it so happens that truth must be spoken where it can be spoken. The earliest preachers were especially charged, when persecuted in one city, to flee to another. If the slave States will not endure to be told of their sins, by men living within their own borders, it becomes necessary to teach them from some other standpoint. We do not go into taverns and distilleries to lecture on temperance, nor into infidel club rooms to preach the gospel. Yet lecturing and preaching are useful, notwithstanding we are unable at first to reach directly the most guilty. According to the objection above stated, Christ, when he came to establish the gospel, should have appeared, not in Judea, where there was some knowledge of the true God, but in the darkest regions of paganism. Why did he not go at first where there was least light? Plainly, because there was less prospect of success. For the same reason, the anti-slavery movement must be confined, in its incipiency, to places where there is some light—where the principles of civil liberty are well enough understood and sufficiently appreciated, to serve as a stepping stone to the new platform. Why did not Washington and Jefferson go to England to inculcate their republican and revolutionary doctrines? Doubtless they thought it better to make the effort here, where revolution and republicanism were more congenial to the public mind. They found opposition enough even here, and so does the anti-slavery cause in the free States.

It is well known that many slave-holders thirst for the blood of those who oppose slavery, and it is only justifiable prudence to avoid their rage so long as we can, without retarding the progress of truth. We have the highest authority for this careful regard to personal safety, while battling with the errors of wicked men. "After these things Jesus walked in Galilee; for he would not walk in Jewry, because the Jews sought to kill him."

Although we have no slaves or slave-holders in this region, we have great numbers of people who need enlightening on the subject, in order to discharge their duty. If they remain ignorant of slavery, we shall look in vain for them to aid, by precept or example, when the Church and the Government undertake to put down the evil. Ignorance is weakness; not to know the horrors of slavery, is to be feeble in opposing it. Again, if slave-holders perceive that non-slave-holders are ignorant and indifferent on the subject, they will construe this indifference into positive approval, and hold on their way. Finding that the practice of slavery does not sink them in the estimation of mankind, they will be confirmed in the vice: whereas, if they see themselves branded with infamy and treated as pirates, they will naturally pay some respect to the opinions of the world, and such as desire to be respectable, will quit the abominable business. Another reason for discussing slavery in the free States is, that the Churches and the Government, as things now are, accord to the institution their support. We have no slaves, but we are willing that others should have them. We give our sanction to slavery, by not entering our protest against it. This is holding slaves indirectly. We would quite as soon do the wrong, as give countenance to those who do it. It is an old maxim, that the partaker is as bad as the thief. The accessory is no better than the principal.

CHAPTER VIII.

NO MIDDLE GROUND — THE CHURCH MUST EITHER ABOLISH SLAVERY OR ADOPT IT.

A MIDDLE course — partly sanctioning and partly repudiating the system of slavery—has been advocated by some, and is by them supposed to be that pursued by the apostles. Among the more recent advocates of this position, is Dr. Bond, the editor of the Christian Advocate and Journal. He claims that the M. E. Church stands upon this basis. The following is his statement:

"We took also the ground that the position of the Methodist Episcopal Church was now precisely the same with the apostolic Church, in regard to slave-holders; that the apostles did not make emancipation a condition of Church-fellowship, although slaves abounded in the Roman Empire, where they planted the gospel personally. Not a single command to this effect can be found in their letters to the Churches, while obedience to masters is enjoined upon slaves in the strongest terms. But did the apostles therefore sanction the *system* of slavery which prevailed in their day? Surely they did not; nor did those they gathered into the fold of Christ so understand them."

This extract contains a remarkable statement, but whether tenable or not, will shortly appear. It affirms that "the position of the M. E. Church is now precisely the same with the apostolic Church, in regard to slave-holders." If this be so, then it follows that the apostolic Church had a discipline in which this question occurred, "What shall be done for the extirpation of the evil of slavery?" And the answer to this question must have read thus, "We declare that we are as much as ever convinced of the great evil of slavery; therefore, no slave-holder shall be eligible to any official station in our Church hereafter, where the laws of the State in which he lives will admit of emancipation, and permit the liberated slave to enjoy freedom." This, and much more, together with a rule forbidding "the buying and selling of men, women and children, with an intention to enslave them." If the Doctor cannot admit this, he will please abandon his position, that the Methodist Episcopal Church now occupies, in reference to slave-holders, precisely the same ground as the apostolic Church.

But he further says, "that the apostles did not make emancipation a condition of Church-fellowship." Neither did they make abstinence from any other crimes a condition of Church-fellowship. Nothing is said of murder, perjury, burglary, counterfeiting, and are we to understand that because these are not specifically prohibited, men who commit such things are suitable for Church-membership? These crimes probably "abounded in the Roman Empire, where they planted the gospel personally," yet nothing is said about excluding such culprits from the Church: "not a single command to this effect can be found in their letters to the Churches." Now we contend that emancipation might be omitted for the same reason that operated in the latter case — that is, because the enumeration of so palpable a duty was superfluous. Christianity aimed to establish universal holiness, and it was quite sufficient to lay down the rule, and cite a few cases, as mere illustrations of its application. A system which teaches that it is wrong to steal even the smallest sum, surely cannot be considered as teaching that it is right to steal a thousand dollars. Nor do we need an express rule on the subject. So of emancipation. No express prohibition was necessary, because the general law of doing good, and only good to our fellow men, included this as well as all other blessings which the master had power to bestow on his slaves.

It appears also that " obedience to masters is enjoined upon slaves in the strongest terms." But any inference drawn from this in favor of slavery would be as absurd as to suppose that an exhortation addressed to laborers absolved their employer from all obligation to pay them their wages. The slave's duty was one thing, and his master's another. Christianity inculcates fidelity in every relation of life, and even kindness towards the wicked; but this does not at all justify the wicked, nor authorize them to continue on in their course. Commanding the slave to be faithful, is no approbation of slave-holding. If it were, then the command to him that is smitten on one cheek to turn the other for the next blow, is an approval of smiting.

Again, " did the apostles therefore sanction the system of slavery which prevailed in their day? Surely they did not." We fully agree with him in this conclusion. His mistake lies in assuming that the apostles did not make emancipation a condition of Church fellowship in fact, because they did not do it in form. He takes for granted that what is not specifically commanded, is not commanded at all. But we maintain that no specific injunction was necessary, inasmuch as the entire system of Christianity was diametrically opposed to slavery, and in favor of emancipation. Yet on this slender and deceitful foundation — the absence of a formal precept — it is vainly attempted to build up a system of religious slave-holding. As well might we erect thereon a system of sanctified piracy, because piracy is not specifically condemned in the New Testament.

If the apostles did not "sanction the system of slavery as it prevailed in their day," they surely did not sanction it in any form, nor at any time. We have no right to infer that they sanctioned some other form of slavery, and, above all, have we no right to get up a form of slavery which we think the apostles would have sanctioned, and palm this upon the world as a scriptural institution. The slavery of those days was, in substance, the slavery of all time; and improve the institution as we may, it will always exhibit, in greater or less degree, the same diabolical features. The system defies all essential modification—it may be destroyed, but cannot be reformed.

If we strike at the master's supremacy by limiting the slave's obedience to such commands as are conformable to the law of God, slavery is at an end—for, in that case, the slave is constituted the judge of his master's commands, the law of God, and his own duty. What he judges to be contrary to right, he is under obligation not to perform. He is in fact free—as free as any man living. But if this element of slavery is suffered to continue, all freedom is out of the question: the master assumes the place of God, and the slave is not permitted to have a conscience. We may suppose that his master is a good man, and will exact nothing wrong of him; but this does not vary the case, for the simple reason that we have no right to give up our consciences to the keeping of even good men. The master cannot answer for his slave at the Judgment; "for every one of us shall give account of himself to God." This necessity of answering for himself at the bar of God, obliges every man to act an independent part — and the slave as much as other men. Good men may err, but if they were infallible, they should not be blindly followed. Our own faculties were intended to be brought into exercise, and should therefore be allowed to choose between good and evil. The slave, in order to be anything more than a machine, must occupy the position of a moral agent. Yet it is utterly impossible that he should be a moral agent and still be a slave. The slave code divests him of all power to think and act for himself, and commits the determination of his conduct wholly to his master, whoever and whatever he may be. No exception is made, or can be made, in favor of any right of conscience; the fact that the slave is a moral being is totally ignored. The same is true of the slave, intellectually. There is no right of private judgment — no recognition of intellectual character. In all these respects the slave is on the same level with the horse or the ox. And the law is perhaps as favorable as it possibly can be under the circumstances; its aim is to give the master "entire control," and this could not be done if the slave were recognized as a man, or permitted to judge for himself in anything. Hence, while we have slavery at all, we must have it with every shade of ancient and modern barbarity. Deeper tinged at times it may be, through the accumulation of superfluous wickedness; but no variations can ever change its essential character. It may cease to exist, but cannot cease to be evil while it exists.

If we strike at the property aspect of slavery, we find the system equally unimprovable. This fact is well shown by Mr. Goodell, in his late valuable work on the American Slave Code:

" The slave cannot be considered by the Government as entitled to its protection while he is not regarded by it as having any rights to be protected. And the Government that recognizes and protects slave chattelhood has already, in that very act, denied to the slave the possession of any rights, by denying to him the right of *self-ownership*, which is the foundation and parent stock of all other rights, and without which they cannot exist.

" Having no right to himself, to his bones, muscles, and intellect, (being all of them the property of his " owner,") he has no right to his own industry, to its wages, or its products ; no right to property or capability of possessing it, as already shown. Of course he has no *rights of property* to be protected by the Government, and none of the rights that grow out of them.

" Having no recognized right of making any contract, he has no contracts with others to be enforced by the Government, and no one has any legal pecuniary claims upon him to be enforced. He can neither sue nor be sued. This is no arbitrary rule. It is the inevitable result of his chattelhood.

" Unable to contract marriage, as already seen, he can bring no action at law against the violator of his bed. Having no marital or parental rights, he has none for the Government to protect.

" Not being accounted a person, but a thing, he can have no personal rights to be protected — no rights of reputation or character — no right to education — no rights of conscience — no rights of personal security — no social rights — no political capabilities or rights — not even the right of petition, as the Federal Congress (very consistently with its recognition of legal human chattelhood) have affirmed.   It would be an anomaly to receive the testimony of such an one in a Court of law !

" It is futile, it is absurd, it is self-contradictory, it is short-sighted and foolish (to say nothing more severe) for any persons to find fault with any of these things, while they recognize as innocent and valid " *the legal relation of master and slave,*" the relation of *slave-ownership*, which includes, implies, and necessitates it all.   Such persons should ask themselves seriously what they *would* have ?

" Would they have the Government stultify itself, and add mockery to injustice by pretending to attempt known impossibilities in the enactment of contradictions ? by making a show of civil protection where none is intended, or where they have rendered it impossible ?   What protection *can* they bestow so long as, by sustaining or even permitting or tolerating human chattelhood, *or failing to suppress it as a crime*, they leave not the slave the possession of one single right of humanity *to be* protected ?

" Or, suppose the Government to be honest and successful in its attempts to confer upon the slave *civil rights*, to recognize and treat him as a member and component element of *civil society*.   Suppose it *to protect*, instead of denying these rights — rights of conscience — rights of security — rights of reputation — right to education — free speech — parental rights — marital rights — right of testimony — right to sue and be sued — right to make contracts — rights of property — right to his earnings and products. What would become of the right to slave-ownership, " the legal relation of master and slave? " Would it not vanish and disappear? Assuredly it would." (*Part* i, *Ch.* 1.)

Again, if we attempt reform in the element of servitude, nothing can be effected without annihilating slavery. Take Paley's definition — " an obligation to labor for the benefit of the master, without the contract or consent of the servant" — and before we can place the relation on Christian grounds, we must eliminate all that gives vitality to the slave system. The servant must have a fair compensation for his labors, and be permitted such a choice of labor as is compatible with the rights of conscience. He must also be allowed the right of " consent and contract" far enough to secure the proper distribution of his time and talents on the several objects for which MAN should live. He cannot plod forever in a single direction, without reference to his own welfare, and solely for his master's benefit; because to do so would be to neglect the duty which every man owes to himself, to mankind, and to God. Now it is obvious that servitude thus denuded of its oppressive or anti-Christian traits is no longer slavery — no, it is not slavery even according to Paley, who has cut down the meaning of the term much below its real import. But if the reform is carried still farther, and to the right of choice is added the rights of property, of marriage, and of citizenship, the resemblance to slavery vanishes entirely, and the man, though a servant, is nevertheless free in everything essential to moral character.

The impossibility of getting up a compromise system — midway between slavery and Christianity — is also apparent, from this consideration : Religious slave-holding is just like all other slave-holding, because the law by which alone a slave can be held, is precisely the same, whether administered by a Christian or a man of the world.

No man of common intelligence can dispute that piety has sometimes made the slave law a dead letter. But this is not slave-holding — it is emancipation in fact, if not in form.   On the other hand it is but too evident that where this effect does not occur, and the slave law is not at once practically abrogated by Christianity, the slave gains nothing by being in the hands of a professedly Christian master.   It has never yet been reported of slave-holding Church members that they use their slaves better than other slaveholders do ; nor is there any reason why they should, if it is right to keep men slaves.   Christians are not expected to use their cattle and horses better than common men ; the nature of these animals makes no special demand upon Christian graces.   So is it with the slave.   If it is right to keep him a slave, it is unquestionably right to degrade him — if right to hold him as property, it is right to treat him as property. We treat the horse as a horse — that is, as he was made to be treated ; in like manner, if the Christian may have a slave, that slave can have no claim to be treated as other human beings are treated. A slave should be treated like a slave, and it is altogether unreasonable, if not impossible to hold slaves, and yet not hold them — to practice slavery without the spirit of slavery. The law determines what slavery shall be — the law makes it what it is. There is not one slave law for the Church member and another for the worldling — no, both must hold slaves, if they hold them at all, by the same law. This law will take effect impartially — it will cut off every right of the slave and reduce him to just as low a level for the Christian as for the infidel. Wherever it operates, one uniform and inevitable result must follow — the man must cease to be a man, and take rank as property, or as a brute. No Christian sympathy can prevent it, no human sagacity elude it. And as the law unmakes the man who ever may be his owner, so it leaves him to the full tide of desolation which slavery pours over the soul. The Christian's property has the same disabilities and liabilities as other men's property; the Christian's brute is just as much a brute as he would be in other hands. In short, the law being the same, the legal and practical evils of slavery are in no wise lessened when the slave is owned by a Christian. It is idle to think that Christian principle can execute such a law — can treat men as slaves — and yet not abuse them.

"Slaves as a class cannot be treated kindly. We might as well say a person was run over by a wagon, and had both legs crushed mildly. The wheels of slavery cannot crush human hearts with mild force. It is the force of hell — it burns while it strikes." (*N. Y. Tribune, May* 18, 1853.)

This is the exact truth. No matter who may execute the infernal law — its diabolical effects are ever the same. An angel could not make slaves of men without doing violence to the nature which God has given them.

It has been proposed to modify slavery by restricting its motives. The advocates of this plan think to give slavery a moral character, by excluding from the practice everything mercenary. They propose to treat all who hold slaves for gain, as sinners; while those who hold them for any or all other reasons, are to be esteemed as innocent. But it is rather late in the day to enact that slaves shall not be held for gain, when even slave-holders themselves acknowledge the institution to be an impoverishing affair. The whole south is a monument of desolation produced by slave-holding, and with this sad example staring us in the face, common sense is quite sufficient, without the aid of Church-discipline, to keep us from holding slaves for gain. Wicked men see that the curse of God is on all slave-holders — the very soil on which they live is scathed and blighted, till it bears most unequivocal marks of divine indignation. There is no gain in slavery, and this fact is so well known that the Church need not make any prohibitory rule in that direction. The sum of the matter is this; those who make the above proposition, object to slavery only on one ground — that of gain: whereas it is objectionable on every ground. They leave the Church open to slavery for all reasons save one, and that one, it happens by the providence of God, no slave-holder of common sense would ever think of avowing.

But the effort to distinguish between the two kinds of slave-holders will always be abortive, and a rule excluding only those who hold slaves for gain, will never meet the wants of the Church. It will be impossible to apply it justly, and inconvenient to apply it at all. Slavery allowed in the Church under some circumstances, will remain in the Church under all circumstances. So it has been, and so it ever will be. We do not believe that the attempt to distinguish between those who hold slaves for gain, and those who hold them not for gain, can ever be successful. But if it could, it would not improve the character of slavery. There is a sufficiency of other motives no better than that of gain — as, for instance, laziness, licentiousness, pride and power — and if the practice when based upon these is still tolerated, its character will remain unchanged. The truth, however, is, that no excellency of motives — no peculiarity of circumstances can justify the act. Hence we oppose all slave-holding. We make one single distinction in the case, and but one, namely, that between real and apparent — slave-holding in fact, and slave-holding in form only. There may be nominal or formal Christians who are not real Christians and will not be saved; so also there may be nominal or formal slave-holders who are not real slave-holders, and, therefore, will not be lost. As to any distinction in the character of slave-holders, other than this, we make none.

If the man really holds a slave, we count him a sinner; but if he only appears to hold a slave, and does not hold one in fact, we say he may be a Christian. We place slavery in the category of crimes, and can as little approve of slave-holding when not practiced for gain, as we could of piracy when not practiced for gain.

Since the foregoing was written, a circumstance has occurred which bears with some weight upon a remark or two, and may be thought to enhance the importance of the distinction between holding slaves for gain, and not for gain. Our observation that "slave-holders themselves acknowledge the institution to be an impoverishing affair," was based partly on personal knowledge, and partly on the following from Dr. Bond, who is both a native and a resident of a slave State, and whose extensive opportunities have enabled him to form an opinion every way entitled to respect.

" We have already said that we have never known a Methodist — and we will now add any other Christian — who avowed, or would acknowledge, that he held slaves for gain, or pecuniary profit — no, not even in the most southern States of ' the Union. We have spoken with none on the subject who did not profess to lament the existence of slavery as a great evil, which they were compelled to endure; and for the most part they all admit that the evil is not compensated by pecuniary advantages — that hired labor would be more profitable, if slave labor did not exclude the free; a truth which is abundantly proved by the exhaustion, nay, the absolute denudation of a great portion of the land in the slave-holding States."

But it seems that the progress of things has developed a man, who, in the light of the nineteenth century, is willing to stand up and declare that in his Church slaves are held for gain. At the General Assembly of the (New School) Presbyterian Church, which convened during the last month at Buffalo, one of the members distinctly avowed the principle which we had supposed the retributions of Providence, and respect for the opinions of mankind — if not for the gospel — would forbid any sane man to assume. The N. Y. Tribune thus reports the gentleman:

"Rev. Mr. McLane, of Mississippi, marched up to the mark and 'faced the music' without winking. Such a committee as this which the report contemplates we will not receive. But if you ask how many if our Church members are slave-holders, I answer, all who are able to be. If you ask how many slaves they own, I answer, just as many as their means will permit."

A friend of ours who was on the spot and heard for himself, gives the language in still stronger terms:

"Mr. McLane, a Presbyterian minister from Mississippi, with Southern frankness said: 'We disavow the action of the Detroit Assembly. *We have men in our Churches who buy slaves, and work them,* BECAUSE THEY CAN MAKE MORE MONEY BY IT THAN IN ANY OTHER WAY. *And the more of such men we have the better. All who can, own slaves; and those who cannot, want to.*"

He further adds:

" No Southern man objected to this, at the time, as a wrong statement of the case. But two days after, when McLane had gone home, and when they saw what use was being made of this frank avowal, two men, one from Missouri, and one from Tennessee, said it was not true in their sections. There, the brethren held slaves not for gain, but as an act of benevolence !"

Now, to our mind, there is nothing especially horrible in this acknowledgment, inasmuch as gain is a lawful motive when connected with a lawful business. Slavery is, in every sense secular; slave-breeding, slave-trading, and slave-working, constitute a regular branch of business from which it is impossible to exclude the desire of gain, though we were of opinion that the judgments of God had so blasted the country, and the prospects of those who pursue it, that no one could rationally hope to make it profitable. We thought that slavery had become as many other pursuits in which men continue because they have made large investments, and find it difficult to effect a change, though they are conscious the business is a losing one. It appeared to us that the condition of the Southern States, as contrasted with the Northern States, was enough to make it quite obvious, even to slave-holders, that slavery could only impoverish a nation. But we accept the testimony of Mr. McLane, and correct our statement accordingly. Be it, then, that many, or all the members of Southern Churches hold slaves for gain, rather than for benevolence — they have not fallen in our estimation. To be sure, they avow a less exalted motive, but still an honorable one ; and they might pass as Christians, were slavery under any circumstances compatible with religion. Indeed, there are reasons why we might even prefer that gain should be set forth as the reason for slave-holding. It is more creditable to slave-holders themselves — it shows that they do not affect virtues which all the world knows they do not possess. It is better that practice and profession should correspond ; but they cannot where the latter is benevolence, and the former a congeries of malevolence. Yet, some men, more shameless than others, have the effrontery to say in the light of Heaven, that slavery is a mercy !

But if slave-holding is an act of mercy, we should like to know what is an act of cruelty. What a comment is this argument on society in slave-holding States ! Men must be reduced to a level with brutes as the only means of escaping from a worse fate ! Nay, call it not an escape, for their can be no worse fate. Slavery is worse than death. So will every freeman decide in an instant. Why, then, talk of holding men in chattelhood, in order " to protect them from greater evils ?" We deny the existence of greater evils of a social character, and challenge any man to show that slavery is not " THE SUM OF ALL VIL-LANIES." Those who hold slaves to save them from a worse condition, should know that a worse condition, short of the bottomless pit, is not possible. This idle, worthless, nonsensical plea has too long been tolerated. When a man's rights are all gone, and he finds himself and posterity doomed to perpetual slavery, let him not be insulted, and let not the common sense of mankind be outraged by the declaration that all this has been done to save him from a worse fate — been done in kindness, and with a true intention to fulfil the law of love.   Let the crime stand as a crime, and add not hypocrisy to robbery.   Say, if possible, that it was done for gain, and thus avoid pouring contempt upon the doctrines of HIM who has taught us by example as well as precept, that " we ought to lay down our lives for the brethren."

Upon the whole, we are more than ever convinced that no discrimination of motives can avail anything towards improving the character of slavery, or relieving the Church in any degree from this dreadful incubus. Sinful it is, and sinful it will remain, in spite of the most accommodating casuistry. It must be prohibited entirely, or nothing is done. It is prohibition that we want — not a sublimation of motives. The Church must put away the evil, instead of attempting merely to regulate it. It is not regulation that slavery calls for, but extirpation. The monstrous iniquity is just as well without regulation as with it. Villany is no better for being systematic. We must have the whole or nothing — the institution admits of no amendment, nor does it need any. Slavery is theft, and when the Church opens its door to thieves, she will of course not be particular whether they have stolen little or much.

CHAPTER IX.

CONCLUSION.

WE must now bring this work to a close, but not without a word in vindication of the objects which are ever kept in view by those who truly appreciate this great branch of Christian enterprise.

There are those who — mistaking the genius of Christianity — complain bitterly of the whole anti-slavery movement. They regard it as unauthorized intermeddling, or at best as a mere refinement in morals, alike impracticable in itself and mischievous in its effects. Hence they have no patience with the advocates of emancipation.

If all men of this stamp would bring the question home to themselves, they would be able to judge with more wisdom. Were they chattels personal — were they, together with their wives and children, down to the latest generation, doomed to the auction block — to the rice swamps — to the slave driver's lash — to brutal ignorance — to concubinage — to poverty — to bondage and shame — would they think our feeble efforts extreme? Impossible! It is only because all this burden rests upon other shoulders, that they can so easily bear it. Not an hour — not a moment would they groan under such unrighteous oppression. They would say with the noble Patrick Henry, "Give me liberty, or give me death." But they are quite willing to bind this intolerable load upon others, and make them bear it forever, although they would not themselves touch it with one of their fingers. Were they suffering in this manner, discussion would be to their ears a music sweeter than the Æolian harp. Were they unable to speak, how gladly would they listen to the outbursts of insulted humanity, as it broke forth in impetuous advocacy of their rights! Every philanthropist who stood up to plead their cause, would seem an angel, and every word of condemnation uttered against their oppressors, would sound as if emanating from the throne of eternal justice. It is easy to bear other men's misfortunes, and so long as these men can have all the liberty they want for themselves and theirs, they will not much heed the fact that millions around them have none at all. The story of the slave's wrongs will tire upon their ear, and prove disgusting.

Such, of course, see nothing momentous in the issues of this controversy — nothing at stake of sufficient importance to justify stern effort — nothing that should disturb the peace of the guilty, or enlist the energies of the pure. So trivial is the whole matter, that all attempts to keep the question before the public, are resisted as though anti-slavery was already an effete speculation. Persons of this stamp do not hesitate to declare that the subject is entirely exhausted. But however true it may be that the arguments and resources of these apologists are exhausted, it is not at all true of the slave question. The moral miasma of this great national sin is spreading everywhere, and corrupting the life-blood of the whole country. There is not a single free State, nor a single Church in the land, but what feels the deadly evil creeping to its heart. The subject exhausted! Never! Never till oppression ceases; never till the last slave is free. Tell us not that the subject is exhausted, while more than three millions of human beings in our midst have not the right to worship God or protect their own virtue. Tell it not while these millions — on whom rest all the obligations of humanity — are forbidden to read the Scriptures, denied marriage, and sold like cattle in the market. We envy not the man who can survey this accumulated mass of unrighteousness with indifference. It is no sight for languid solicitudes. These hoary wrongs make no transient appeal to Christian sympathy; they move the heart, and keep it moved till God takes away the evil, or withdraws the blessing of religious sensibility. But it may be said, "this belongs to Cæsar — the Church has nothing to do with the evil." We deny it utterly. The Church has everything to do with slavery, if slavery is sin. Cæsar belongs to Christ. Sins of the State are to be reproved and extirpated as truly as the sins of individuals. It is not enough for the Church to say, "it is the State, it is the State," and deem her own responsibility ended. The State must be rebuked for its wickedness. If our Christianity cannot do this — cannot remonstrate against iniquity in the high places of our own semi-Christian government—how is it fit to grapple with the legalized sins of pagan nations? Our religion is not worth exporting to foreign coun-

tries, if it is thus impotent at home. Exhausted!
Yes, when the kingdom of God has fully come, and
not before. Until that auspicious hour, the Church
must keep her armor on, and push the battle to the
gate.

THE END.